D1568505

JOHN WESLEY HUNT

Mutual Federal Savings & Loan Association
National Industries, Inc. / Rand McNally & Company
Mrs. Victor Sams / Shell Oil Company, Louisville
South Central Bell Telephone Company
Southern Belle Dairy Co. Inc. / Standard Oil Company
Standard Printing Co., H. M. Kessler, President
Thomas Industries Inc. / Mary L. Wiss, M.D.
Younger Woman's Club of St. Matthews

JOHN WESLEY HUNT

Pioneer Merchant, Manufacturer, and Financier

JAMES A. RAMAGE

THE UNIVERSITY PRESS OF KENTUCKY

Research for The Kentucky Bicentennial Bookshelf
is assisted by a grant from the
National Endowment for the Humanities.
Views expressed in the Bookshelf do not
necessarily represent those of the Endowment.

ISBN: 0-8131-0204-9

Library of Congress Catalog Card Number: 74-7881

A statewide cooperative scholarly publishing agency
serving Berea College, Centre College of Kentucky,
Eastern Kentucky University, Georgetown College,
Kentucky Historical Society, Kentucky State University,
Morehead State University, Murray State University,
Northern Kentucky State College, Transylvania University,
University of Kentucky, University of Louisville, and
Western Kentucky University.

Editorial and Sales Offices: Lexington, Kentucky 40506

To Ann

Contents

Acknowledgments   xi

1 / Introduction   1

2 / Disgruntled Partner,
Would-Be Privateer   13

3 / The Pioneer Merchant   21

4 / Racehorses   41

5 / Hemp   54

6 / Hopemont   72

7 / Patriarch   90

Bibliographical Essay   101

Illustrations follow page 56

Acknowledgments

D<small>R</small>. H<small>OLMAN</small> H<small>AMILTON</small> contributed invaluable counsel, stimulating suggestions, and warm friendship. Dr. Mary W. Hargreaves, Dr. James F. Hopkins, and Dr. Carl B. Cone offered helpful criticisms and suggestions when the manuscript was in the form of doctoral dissertation chapters. I express appreciation to Northern Kentucky State College for a research grant which enabled me to broaden the study. Dr. W. Frank Steely has inspired and encouraged me all along the way. Julia Duke Henning gave permission to reproduce the original portrait which belongs to her; Edward James Mathews and the Blue Grass Trust for Historic Preservation permitted the use of reproductions of portraits in their possession; and Joe Munson assisted with photography.

Dr. Jacqueline Bull shared her tremendous knowledge of sources on Kentucky history and was very kind to me during the months when I seemed to be living in the University of Kentucky, library. I am grateful to James R. Bentley of the Filson Club and Roemol Henry of the Transylvania University library for their assistance. I express appreciation to the librarians of the University of Kentucky, the Filson Club, Transylvania University, Kentucky Historical Society, Cincinnati Historical Society, Missouri Historical Society, Mississippi Department of Archives and History, Historical Society of Pennsylvania, American Philosophical Society, and the Free Public Library in Trenton, New Jersey.

Finally and most important, I express deepest appreciation to my wife Ann, who assisted with proofreading and typing and provided gentle, steadfast support.

1

INTRODUCTION

WHEN JOHN WESLEY HUNT rode into the frontier town of Lexington, Kentucky, in July of 1795, he arrived at an excellent time and place to rise in American business, for Lexington was becoming a major commercial center for pioneers moving westward. At twenty-two he was well equipped to seize the opportunity which lay before him on the frontier. For three generations the Hunts had been merchants in New Jersey and John had learned merchandising from his father, Trenton's most prominent merchant. Through the valuable experiences ahead in merchandising, horse breeding, hemp manufacturing, banking, and finance, he was to develop, to an uncommon degree, the ability to predict business trends and to redirect investments at the opportune moment. Psychologically he was ready to face any obstacle and sacrifice any comfort. Making innovations which helped mold the economy of Lexington, the Ohio and Mississippi valleys, and the nation, he became a prototype of the nineteenth-century American entrepreneur. His wealth accumulated to the extent that he was regarded as the first millionaire west of the Alleghenies. A businessman who knew him well was probably not the only one to note that everything he touched turned into gold. One of Lexington's outstanding citizens himself for over fifty years, John founded one of Kentucky's most prominent families; for generations the Hunts and Morgans were leaders in the social, economic, and military life of Kentucky and the nation.

Hunt's family in Trenton sympathized with him about the sacrifice of moving to the frontier. His stepmother wrote: "I enter into your deprived & solitary situation with all the disagreeable reflections it will sometimes occasion & wish with all my heart you was blest with a *good* Wife to lessen, if she could not remove entirely, every ill you have to combat." The comforts of marriage lay ahead, but in 1795 John locked the door at night and slept under the counter in the store. Homesick and lonely, he invited one of his brothers to come live with him and pleaded for more letters from home. Nevertheless, he was where he chose to be. He had failed to make a fortune in a mercantile partnership in Richmond, Virginia, and had failed in commercial shipping in Norfolk. Lexington might be remote from the niceties of the Atlantic coast, but the frontier offered challenge and opportunity.

Standing behind the counter of his general store in Lexington, John looked more like a magistrate than a merchant. Of medium height and broad-shouldered, his build was sturdy, almost heavy. Appearing older than twenty-two, with light brown hair combed back neatly from the broad forehead, with large ears, heavy eyebrows, a very prominent, straight nose and a large mouth, John was not particularly handsome. The light blue eyes burned with intensity and invited one to draw only so near. The firm lips expressed self-assurance and determination. Genuinely interested in others, he was polite and gentlemanly, but no one considered him outgoing. One tended to be awed in his presence. It was almost as though he were looking down from a higher level, judging and demanding respect. His friends learned that he was kind and helpful, and they were comfortable with him; yet there remained a certain distance, an aloofness about Hunt. Little farm girls, already overwhelmed by the smell of spices, dyes, and leather, the shelf-lined walls, and frying pans hanging from the rafters, edged closer to their mothers in response to his "Hello, young ladies!"

The store was clean and orderly; the customer realized immediately that John was master of the business. Familiar with his stock of goods, with exchange rates, markets, and prices, he knew what he was doing. Furthermore, weather-beaten pioneer farmers encountered no effeminate indoorsman when they met Hunt. The large red cheeks, rough hands, and riding boots reminded the customer that John was a superior horseman and horse trader. When he folded his apron for the day and dressed for dinner at one of the nearby taverns, he emerged in the latest Philadelphia fashion. Always careful in dress, in 1795 he wore a dark green broadcloth coat, white waistcoat, light trousers buckled at the knee, white silk stockings, and black slippers. His neatly knotted black cravat set off the ruffled linen shirt with high collar worn flat against the cheeks. With little of the charm and charisma which attracted people to such men as Henry Clay and Aaron Burr, John was not liked as much as he was admired. His manners, the way he dressed, the strength of character in his expression, everything about him inspired respect. He was not the kind of man one slapped on the back—familiarity was reserved for the closest friends and relatives.

Even with his family John was somewhat reserved. His brothers knew how to keep their distance. Hearing that John was more than casually interested in a girl in Lexington, Abraham, Jr., apologized for mentioning it: "Excuse the liberty I have taken with you upon this subject." Longing for any news from home, he scolded his parents and brothers for not writing often. "Father, you write short letters," and "Pearson, write to me as a brother and not as a stranger," he complained. Nevertheless, John was slow to answer the mail he received. "None of the family have had a letter from you for a

3

long time," a brother pointed out. "I have not received one from you since you was here & I have wrote to you several times." His stepmother echoed: "We think of you, we talk of you and write to you but we never have had a line from you since you crossed the Allegany except the one I mentioned."

When John wrote, his letters were frustratingly uncommunicative. Brother Robert complained: "I wish you would in writing to me sometimes descend to the particulars of your situation." Later Robert heard that John was engaged: "All your friends are very well & very particular in their inquiries about your Wife that is to be. Indeed they have had you married some time. I wish you would let a body know something about her besides her Name." It is easy to sympathize with a friend who chided John for his reticence. "Why the Devil have you not ere this given a Sketch of your Journey? Have you seen any shippers or any loud talking men with cocked hats in your absence? Have you seen any little white mares lathered with soap suds? Or in the name of St. Peter what have you seen, heard or done? God bless you, let me hear from you."

Perhaps one reason for John's inattention to his correspondence was his concern for his business. One of his goals in life was to make a large fortune, an ambition which he shared with his brother Wilson, a merchant in Philadelphia. Their stepmother blamed Wilson's permanent state of bachelorhood on his cupidity. "I preach up matrimony to Wilson continually," she commented, "confident no happiness is equal to that shared by man & wife. But he is so desirous of increasing his wealth to such a sum before he can think of it that he may live afterwards in a certain way which he has persuaded himself is essential, that I begin to despair, especially as I fancy he has removed the point he set off to attain more than once." She continued with a lesson for John: "Wealth is a good thing as a means to promote happiness but happiness by no means depends upon it. It is not even a principal source. After a competancy obtain'd, a well-regulated mind will never make accumulating the end of living." In fact, John's motivation was based on something more profound than the desire to acquire a fortune. Possessing the pioneer urge to strike out in new directions, John thrived on challenge, delighted in achievement, and was willing to put in long hours and make sacrifices to succeed.

In addition, John valued the respect of his fellow citizens. In 1792, when he was nineteen and in business in Richmond, Virginia, his father gave advice which he took to heart: "I am well pleased to find that you have every reason to be contented with your situation & that the attention from the People in Richmond has equaled your expectation. In these things everything depends on the manner we conduct ourselves & it is an agreeable reflection to suppose that we are esteemed by our neighbors & this will generally be the case when we conduct ourselves with propriety." John would tolerate no slander against his reputation. A year before he came to Lexington he attempted to trace down a rumor against him. An acquaintance responded to his inquiry: "Your name was mentioned at Mr. Brunels [probably an inn] and some gentleman mentioned you was fond of play, which I never heard before. . . . Mr. MacKenzie therefore is alltogether mistaken if he says that I mentioned you was fond of play. . . . You are at liberty to make any use of this letter you please."

Although little of a gambling man, except in business, John did propose to live life to the full. He enjoyed music, drama, food, wine, lotteries, horses, and the game of chess. He danced, went to teas and parties, joined the Masons and the Episcopal church. The ladies were impressed with his impeccable manners and knowledge of fashion and they were flattered with the attention he gave them. He left a sweetheart named Maria in Trenton and discussed girls with his friends. When he was in Richmond, Charles Higbee wrote: "Let me know the news of your City, and do not be afraid of saying too much of the sweet Miss R——. I beg you will present my best love to *her*, particularly tell her I love [her] more than ever." After John settled in Lexington it was common knowledge in the family that he was looking for a wife. On January 1, 1796, brother Wilson greeted: "I wish you happy new year, and an amiable wife before the end of it." However, the most important thing in life for John was business; nothing excited him as much as a profitable new business venture.

Walking the streets of Lexington for the first time, John must have been impressed with the noisy, bustling atmosphere. First settled in 1779, the town expanded little until the mid-1790s. In 1795 it was fast becoming the largest, busiest, and most civilized town west of the Allegheny Mountains. In spite of the fact that Lexington was not located on a navigable stream, it became the trading center for most of Kentucky. Nearly all early Kentucky roads passed through the town. The Wilderness Road carried pioneers moving westward into Lexington, and people descending the Ohio on their way to points south of this river disembarked at Limestone (now Maysville) and traveled overland, passing through the Bluegrass community. There they obtained supplies for settling on the frontier. Many remained to farm in the region and for them Lexington became not only the supplier of eastern goods but also the major dispatching center for farm products shipped by river to New Orleans. In the mid-1790s the westward flow of pioneers was increasing, and Lexington was growing. The population expanded from 835 in 1790 to 1,797 in 1800. In the latter year, Pittsburgh had but 1,565 people and Cincinnati 500. In 1795 Lexington's nearly 300 log and frame houses were beginning to be replaced by brick structures. The streets were in a gridiron pattern, with Main Street running parallel and to the north of the Town Branch of Elkhorn Creek. Main Street was eighty-two feet wide; the remaining streets were narrower—yet a visitor thought them "sufficiently large." There was a stone courthouse on the two-acre public square; and the trustees were sponsoring construction of a market house "60 feet long and 25 feet wide with pillars of Brick, and a joint Shingle roof."

The trustees of Lexington were attempting to bring a measure of civilization to the streets. No longer were hogs allowed to run at large in the town. Horse racing in the streets was forbidden and studhorses could be shown to potential customers only on Water Street below Cross Street. For nearly a year horse racks and the hitching of horses in the streets had been forbidden. Slaughterhouses were forced to clean their premises when the odor became a nuisance. Porches and fences reaching into the streets were removed. The owners of lots on Main Street were warned to drain off the stagnant water which had collected on their property. Hunt had been in Lexington less than a month when the trustees prohibited washing clothes at the public springs.

Transylvania Seminary had a plain two-story brick building facing Second Street, on the "college lawn." In 1798 the Seminary would merge with Kentucky Academy; and the following year, with the addition of law and medical departments, the institution became the first university in the West. In 1795 there was a "School for the Instruction of Young Ladies" and on Tates Creek Road eleven miles from Lexington, a boarding school opened its doors. The sum of $500 was raised by public subscription for the purpose of establishing a public library; in January, 1796, the first 400 volumes would arrive. In the meantime, works such as *Paradise Lost, Tom Jones, Rights of Woman,* David Hume's *History of England,* and Blackstone's *Commentaries* could be purchased at John Bradford's bookstore.

The less contemplative pioneer could visit one of the several taverns or billiard parlors. On Short Street, next door to Captain McCoy's Billiard Table, a "House of Entertainment" offered the "choicest of liquors" and advertised, "Select companies may be accommodated with private rooms, and dinner or supper on the shortest notice." By 1800 Lexington would have two newspapers, churches, debating clubs, musical and drama societies, jockey clubs, and facilities for horse racing and dancing. Indeed, the town was becoming known as the Athens of the West.

Hunt was doubtless most interested in the retail businesses of the town. At least thirteen local general stores advertised in the *Kentucky Gazette* from June to August of 1795. A month before John arrived, William West had opened a store next door to Walter Taylor's tavern. Robert Barr was in business on Main Street at the "sign of the Spinning Wheel, adjoining the two locust trees." Alexander and James Parker, in their stand across from the courthouse, offered merchandise for cash or hides. Benjamin Stout, next door to Henry Marshall's tavern, was trading goods for "Cash, Whiskey, Bear Skins and country made Sugar." In addition several craftsmen sold their goods in specialty shops. There was a clock- and watchmaker, a gold- and silversmith, a coppersmith, a hatter, a bookbinder and paper supplier, a wheel- and chairmaker, a saddler, and at least one shoemaker. Thomas Hart advertised that he had begun the manufacture of cordage and was paying cash or merchandise for good clean hemp. Hunt had several competitors in the mercantile trade but the market was expanding enough to make the business profitable.

John had grown up in a general store like the one he operated in Lexington. The Hunt family in America descended from Ralph Hunt, who emigrated from England in 1656 and helped found a settlement at Newtown, Long Island. Ralph was surveyor of Indian lands and lieutenant of the militia for Newtown. Around the turn of the century the Hunts moved to New Jersey and Wilson Hunt, born in 1715, lived there all his life. Wilson bred horses, operated a grist mill, farmed, and served as collector of Hunterdon County. When Wilson died in 1782 he left an estate valued at £2,496, a sizable fortune.

Abraham Hunt, Wilson's son, also engaged in horse trading and milling. In 1777 he advertised to sell "two elegant full blooded Stallions, one called Bajazet & the other Juniper: They are both good bays, and fifteen hands high." And in 1793 Abraham expressed pride in his grist mill: "Our Mill is in excellent Order, one pair of Stones grinds faster than any thing I have seen." Abraham's main interest, however, was the merchandising business which he established in Trenton. To the farmers of central New Jersey he furnished goods imported from abroad in return for wheat, pork, beef, apples, rye, and corn. Abraham also sold goods wholesale to local retailers in the surrounding area. In 1778 he and his partner, Moore Furman, advertised to sell "West-India Rum by the hogshead or gallon, Geneva, Apple Brandy and Whiskey by the barrel or gallon; and a few chests best Bohea Tea."

Like many other important merchants, Abraham Hunt was a community leader. He was postmaster of Trenton for six years. He served on the board of trustees of Trenton's Presbyterian Church for fifty-seven years. Before the Revolution, Abraham was a member of the local committee of correspondence. During the Revolution he held a commission as lieutenant colonel of militia and he disbursed government funds. When Trenton was incorporated in 1792 he was chosen one of its first aldermen.

On Christmas night in 1776 Abraham Hunt made a rather unusual contribution to the patriot war effort. He invited Colonel Johann Rall, commander of British forces in Trenton, and several of his associates to a Christmas dinner in his home. After supper Hunt brought up the finest wine in his cellar and the festivities continued into the early morning hours of December 26. Outside the night was dark and cold. At about eleven o'clock snow began falling on a body of American troops on the Delaware River, a few miles north of town. General George Washington was moving his forces across the river in preparation for a surprise attack on Trenton. By 3:00 A.M., all of Washington's men were on the New Jersey side of the Delaware. At dawn they attacked and won a great victory. Abraham Hunt had contributed to the surprise by preparing the enemy officers for a very restful night. There is no record of whether or not he had foreknowledge of the coming attack. He may have been as surprised as the British, but being an American patriot, he was pleased at the outcome.

Abraham Hunt married Theodosia Pearson, a daughter of Robert Pearson, justice of the quorum for Burlington County. Abraham and Theodosia named their third child, born in August 1773, John Wesley Hunt. John had two older brothers, Pearson and Wilson; Theodore, Abraham, Jr., Robert, Theodosia, and Philemon were younger. When John was ten their mother died. Her tombstone declared that she had been so cheerful and gentle that "she never made an enemy, nor ever lost a friend. To know her once, was to love her forever." Abraham took a second wife, Mary Dagworthy, and they had a son and daughter, both of whom died at an early age.

John appears to have been very close to his New Jersey family. He and his father seem to have understood each other particularly well. At crucial periods in his life John wrote him for advice, knowing that the answer he received would be full of the wisdom of experience and tempered by good-natured regard. The letters John received from his brothers and sister after he left home reveal that they had genuine affection and concern for each other. Sister Theodosia's were an absolute delight. In February 1793 she told brother "Johnny" about her dancing school. A Mr. Dilling had come to the Hunt household recruiting pupils and charmed Mrs. Hunt into agreeing to allow Theodosia, Theodore, and Philemon to attend if Mr. Hunt did not object. Then Dilling called on Mr. Hunt in the store and led him to think that Mrs. Hunt had already consented. Dilling's dance classes went smoothly for three days, but on the fourth he was "drunk as a piper," and on the fifth he went for a ride and did not return for two weeks.

Perhaps Theodosia acquired her witty and playful nature from her contact with John's stepmother Mary. On the family's luck in a lottery, Mary reported: "Our Tickets, O John what unlucky creatures we are! One a blank the other a prize of five Doll. only, Abr'am a blank." Sometimes she gossiped: "Jimmy Mott and Nancy go on as usual very slow in their approaches to matrimony, but there it must end." In February 1793 nearly all of the family friends and relatives in Philadelphia visited the Hunts in Trenton. Several of them took advantage of the snow by traveling in a sleigh. With a house full of guests, Mary remarked that they "must find their way down by some other mode of conveyance for the chief ingredient to make Sleying agreeable has entirely disappear'd during the last twenty four hours— In short they are left upon bare ground."

Abraham Hunt's house and store were located in the same two-story building on the corner of King and Second streets in Trenton; to the merchant's sons, the store was as familiar as the parlor. Home life was filled with buying and selling, loading and unloading, and the coming and going of customers. Cases of penknives and barrels of shoes made in England had to be opened. A boy could sit on a chest of black tea grown in China and watch the clerks place cloth produced in India on the shelf. There was always the hope that a box of chocolate would break open or that his father would permit a handful of raisins or almonds. It was the kind of life that could inspire a boy to dream of far away places and of being the master of a store of his own. Occasionally there were visits to Philadelphia, where young John Wesley Hunt watched the ships setting out for distant places and dreamed of owning his own ship and plying the overseas trade.

2

DISGRUNTLED PARTNER, WOULD-BE PRIVATEER

DURING THE PERIOD in which the Hunt children grew up, education (except in New England) was primarily the responsibility of parents. More than likely, the boys and Theodosia received elementary and secondary training from private teachers. According to Mary Hunt, Theodosia's dance teacher (Mr. Dilling) also taught other subjects and had scholars in Burlington in addition to the group of thirty-three at Trenton. The studies of the oldest boys were probably oriented toward mathematics and accounting, and it seems logical to suppose that they served periods of apprenticeship in the Hunt store, because all three entered the mercantile business when they left home. It is certain that John worked in the store and that Abraham, Jr., served an apprenticeship there. Two of the younger brothers attended college. Robert was graduated from Princeton, studied law in Trenton, and was admitted to the bar in New Jersey. Philemon also attended Princeton and in 1800 had the high score in his class examinations. John does not seem to have been academically inclined, and there appears to be no record that he went to college.

Instead in the latter part of 1792, at nineteen years of age, John entered partnership in a mercantile enterprise in Richmond, Virginia, the major export center for tobacco grown in the piedmont of Virginia and the northern part of North Carolina. Farmers also shipped wheat, corn, and livestock to the town, which was developing into an important milling center. Hunt and his senior partner, Harry Heth, purchased general merchandise in Philadelphia for wholesaling and retailing in exchange for wheat. On the side, Heth and Hunt dealt in horses. When he went to Philadelphia in February 1793, Hunt took a studhorse and a number of other horses for sale.

For some reason John quickly became dissatisfied with the partnership. It had not been in effect six months when he informed his father that he planned to separate from Heth and invest heavily in the milling business. Abraham advised him to stay with Heth, writing: "A partnership dissolved in a short time will not do credit to either of you. I wish you would reflect seriously on this Business. From what you have told me yourself, I am sure you must be doing very well, as much so as you had any right to expect. . . . Proceed on your Business as usual, is my wish & advice & the part that I think is prudent for you to act." The partnership continued for several months.

During the summer of 1793 John traveled to the West Indies. It is possible that he accompanied a cargo of flour for sale by the firm; but assuming that he did, it was still unusual for a merchant in his type of business to leave busy day-to-day operations to go on such a voyage. He was probably searching out contacts and gaining knowledge in preparation for a venture in the maritime trade, for early in 1794 he dissolved the partnership with Heth in Richmond and entered the shipping business in Norfolk.

No doubt twenty-year-old Hunt had observed that the American carrying trade was in a period of remarkable expansion. War had begun in Europe. European vessels were drawn off from the belligerents' carrying trade for military use, and ships flying the neutral American flag sailed in to fill the gap. The American reexport trade increased steadily for several years after 1790. Norfolk shared fully in the shipping boom. Before the break with England, businessmen there had a prosperous trade with the British West Indies. Located nearer the West Indies than most major continental ports, Norfolk had provisions and lumber which the islanders were eager to acquire in exchange for sugar, molasses, and rum. The war in Europe contributed to the revival of this exchange.

In his shipping venture, Hunt united with Captain John Cooper, a Frenchman who had been reported to United States authorities in 1793 for commanding a French privateer outfitted in the United States. Harry Heth invested in the company, and possibly there were other investors. The company purchased a merchant vessel which set sail from Norfolk sometime in February of 1794.

Hunt was soon to learn firsthand that neutral shippers ran high risks in the 1790s. Great Britain, endeavoring to starve France into submission, had authorized the capture of all ships carrying provisions to or produce from French islands. When British naval commanders in the Caribbean received these orders early in 1794, the area was crowded with American vessels, including Hunt's, which were doing just that. The British captured 250 American ships by March 1 and 307 by July 31, 1794. One hundred fifty of the vessels detained by March 1 were condemned, and their crews were left stranded. John's vessel was in this group.

The American public was outraged when news of this violation of neutral rights reached the United States. From the beginning of the war many Americans had favored France, the nation which had aided the United States in the Revolution. In Norfolk, where Hunt was living, sentiment was divided but there was strong pro-French feeling; in January 1793, for example, the guns at the fort were fired to celebrate the French victory at

Valmy. In Philadelphia about 2,000 people demonstrated in the streets against the 1794 British seizures. John's older brother Wilson, not realizing that John's interest was involved, wrote from that city: "The D——n British privateers have taken our Vessels." Hunt's friend Joseph Higbee, also in Philadelphia, assured him: "There is no Person who feels more sensibly, than I do, the repeated Insults we are daily experiencing at the hand of that haughty and insolent nation, the British."

John's oldest brother Pearson advised him to rest assured that the government would redress him. Indeed in the spring of 1794 it seemed that the nation was headed for war against Great Britain. On March 26 Congress enacted a thirty-day embargo on foreign trade and later renewed it for a second thirty-day period. The major purpose of the embargo was to cut off food supplies to the British West Indies, which were being used as a base for attacks on the French Caribbean islands. On March 27 Congressman Jonathan Dayton of New Jersey called for the sequestration of American debts to British merchants, the money to be used to pay American losses resulting from British captures. In April a bill providing nonintercourse with Britain came very close to passing. The House approved, while in the Senate only the tie-breaking vote of Vice-President John Adams defeated the measure. However the tension was relieved when British policy was modified in favor of neutrals. The danger of war passed for the time being when President Washington appointed Chief Justice John Jay as minister plenipotentiary to Great Britain in April.

Certainly no one could have been more upset by the British captures than John. Neither the public demonstrations nor the government protests restored his ship. During the sixty-day embargo he committed himself to a course of action which he expected would enable him to recoup his losses, make a fortune, and gain wonderfully satisfying revenge at the same time. British naval vessels and privateers had captured and condemned his merchantman, therefore he would outfit a French privateer and put it out to sea to seize British commercial ships.

There was one great drawback to the scheme—it violated American neutrality. On April 22, 1793, President Washington, with the approval of the Cabinet, had proclaimed that the United States was neutral in the European war. He had warned American citizens to avoid all acts and proceedings which might contravene this position. When Edmond Genêt, French Minister to the United States, commissioned privateers to be outfitted in American harbors, and they began to bring prizes into United States ports, the Washington administration demanded Genêt's recall and withdrew the right of asylum of French privateers. There was no American navy, and the army was on the frontier. Therefore Secretary of the Treasury Alexander Hamilton instructed Treasury agents to report the presence in American ports of privateers fitted out in the United States to the appropriate state governor. State governors were authorized to call out the state militia if necessary to enforce American neutrality. Congress approved the policy and procedure with a law passed on June 5, 1794, which provided punishment for anyone concerned with the fitting out and arming of ships of war and authorized the state militia to serve as an enforcing agent. Hunt's privateering plans clearly contravened American neutrality and, after June 5, violated federal law.

Yet Hunt's partner, the Frenchman John Cooper, had little respect for the neutrality of the United States. In August 1793 he had outfitted a privateer in this country and had been reported to the federal authorities. It is impossible to determine the extent of Cooper's influence on John's decision to enter privateering. Perhaps it was great. The fact that Cooper had a reputation for privateering raises the question of whether Hunt had contemplated that activity from the beginning of their relationship. But there is no available evidence to indicate that Hunt planned anything other than legitimate and legal shipping until after the seizure of his ship.

The apprehension of John's relatives in Trenton and Philadelphia increased as they gradually learned of the new project. They disapproved of Cooper from the beginning. Pearson Hunt informed John: "We are told you are connected with some person who does not stand very high." He cautioned that in dealing with a man "not of the First Character," John might not share the profits equally and had everything to lose in reputation. After Wilson Hunt became acquainted with some of the details of the venture, he urged John to sell part of the ship. If she should be successful, a small share of the profit would be a large sum; if she failed, John's loss would not be so great. "I am sure, you will acknowledge, it is imprudent, and indiscreet, to risk all in one ship," he advised. Pearson argued that the plan was too large for the capital available and concerning the propriety of the enterprise he warned:

C— as a frenchman has an undoubted right to engage in any scheme of the kind but put the question to yourself. As a man of Honour how can you reconcile the scheme? Your country is not-at-War with the one upon which your Gains must bend. . . . Don't from a mistaken notion plunge yourself into difficulties which may injure you materially and perhaps raise doubts in the public sentiment as to the propriety of your Conduct; for if it was generally known here that you had engaged in a plan of this sort, your Credit would be ruined.

John's stepmother categorically condemned privateering: "Privateering, even when sanction'd by a War is but a lisence to plunder & rob individuals." Admonishing again that wealth does not bring happiness, she advised John that he would be better off without a large fortune if he had to sacrifice self-respect and reputation to gain it.

Proceeding with their plan during the sixty-day em-

3

THE PIONEER
MERCHANT

IN THE SPRING of 1795 John Wesley Hunt's cousin, Abijah Hunt, offered a fresh start, a new beginning on the frontier. Abijah, a merchant in Cincinnati, proposed entering partnership with John in a general store to be established in Lexington, Kentucky. Abijah and other pioneer merchants were rising to prosperity on the crest of a wave of westward expansion. For twenty years settlers had migrated across the Alleghenies, but after the defeat of the Indians of the Northwest Territory in 1794 pioneers began streaming down the Ohio River and over the Wilderness Road in increasing numbers.

When the settlers disembarked at Cincinnati or passed through Lexington or other frontier towns, they needed hardware, groceries, and dry goods. Pioneer merchants met this demand. At considerable risk and difficulty, they purchased goods in Philadelphia and other towns on the coast, conveyed them by wagon to Pittsburgh, and then boated them down the Ohio. When local farmers passed the subsistence level and had crops for export, the merchants opened markets for farm crops. They supplied credit and exchange. Thus the merchants were an integral part of frontier economic life.

Many pioneer merchants were entrepreneurs and innovators, new men starting new business ventures. On the frontier, roles were relatively undefined; patterns and habits were yet to be established. Therefore opportunities for innovation were great. The frontier economic world was dynamic, and many pioneer merchants were willing to challenge custom and habit to the disregard of physical obstruction and personal sacrifice. Their delight was challenge; their pleasure accomplishment. Success was their ideal. Many entrepreneurial merchants accumulated capital and then moved into manufacturing. Hunt was one of the most successful entrepreneurs of his time.

Like many pioneer merchants, Hunt first established himself as a junior partner with an established businessman. At twenty-two years of age, John was fortunate in having Abijah Hunt as a partner. Abijah had connections and credit in Philadelphia as well as in the West. From the time Cincinnati was settled in 1788, Abijah's brother Jesse had been in business there. Abijah himself had been in the town for at least two years. Since 1793 "A. Hunt & Co." had operated a tannery and general store in the settlement. In 1795 another brother, Jeremiah, moved from New Jersey to join Jesse and Abijah.

The Cincinnati connection gave John an advantage which most of his competitors in Lexington did not have. Situated at the northern bend of the Ohio River, Cincinnati became the major disembarking point for settlers headed for the interior regions north of the river. Of greater significance in the 1790s, the town was the site of Fort Washington, the major outpost for protection of the Ohio country from the Indians. Army expeditions against the Indians of the Northwest Territory originated in Fort Washington. Abijah and other Cincinnati merchants furnished them provisions. Josiah Harmar's campaign of 1790 originated here, as did Arthur St. Clair's disastrous expedition of 1791 and Anthony Wayne's victorious campaign of 1794. With the defeat of the Indians at the Battle of Fallen Timbers in August

1794, peace was brought to the territory, but Cincinnati remained an important outfitting post for the Western frontier.

In 1795, with the westward flow of immigrants rapidly increasing, Abijah considered the time right for expansion into Kentucky. In Trenton on April 29, 1795, he had a long talk with his cousin John concerning a partnership. After further thought on the matter, Abijah wrote John from Philadelphia the next day making a formal proposal. The partners would be equal and each would put up £1,000 or $2,660.* In Philadelphia Abijah would purchase merchandise valued at £8,000 wholesale, and John would arrange its transportation to Lexington and receive it there. Assisted by two clerks (one acquainted with commerce in Lexington), John would place himself behind the counter. The partners were to share equally in the profits, and, except for the initial purchase, John was to manage the business.

Abijah and his brothers would be situated at Fort Washington and could take in farm produce for goods there. Abijah had just been informed by his intimate acquaintance, Caleb Swan, Paymaster General of the Army, that goods shipped from Philadelphia in May would arrive in Kentucky in time to take a portion of a payment of $160,000 made to the volunteers of Wayne's recent expedition. Abijah expected a net profit of 50 percent for sales in Lexington but estimated that a clear profit over-all would be about 40 percent. In a postscript he stated that $2,000 from John would be sufficient. He instructed John to report to Philadelphia immediately if the proposal met his approval. Obviously it did, because

* The official exchange rate was $4.44 for one pound sterling. However, Hunt's accounts clearly demonstrate that on the domestic market, the rate in the 1790s was $2.66 for one pound. Through 1805 most of Hunt's accounts were still in pounds, except those involving New Orleans, which were in dollars. In 1810 several accounts listed both pounds and dollars and by 1816, pounds had gone out of use completely.

on the following day—May 1, 1795—articles of agreement were drawn up in Philadelphia. Each partner put up $2,000; John was to conduct the business with the help of one clerk (instead of the two proposed earlier) furnished by Abijah; the term was the standard one of three years.

Between May 11 and May 30, 1795, Abijah made purchases from at least twenty-four different wholesale firms in Philadelphia. John probably went along to receive instruction in the business of buying assorted goods which would sell in the western country. By far the largest order was with John's brother Wilson—£1,347 worth of muslins, linens, men's and women's hose, gloves, pantaloons, and other dry goods. Aside from this patronage of Wilson the purchasers shopped around for low prices, favorable terms of credit, and well-assorted quality merchandise. The invoices reveal a good deal of specialization on the part of the wholesalers. There were Bohea and Hyson tea, sugar, coffee, and other groceries from Whelen & Miller; books from Mathew Carey; shoes from Henry Manly; feathers from John D. Blanchard; and pills, drugs, and ointments from Goldthwait & Moore.

Eastern wholesale companies usually granted six months' credit without interest and then charged 6 to 10 percent interest for the next six months, with payment due twelve months from the date of purchase. Invoices of later purchases by the Hunts mostly conform to the general rule. The invoices of May 1795, however, either do not mention the terms or note that payment was due in six months. Merchandise bound for Lexington from Philadelphia was conveyed 320 miles by wagon to Pittsburgh, boated down the Ohio 400 miles to Limestone, and wagoned 65 miles to Lexington. The transportation of Hunt's goods on this route in the summer of 1795 took something less than fifty-six days. He preceded the goods, arranging to have them forwarded at Pittsburgh and Limestone. By July 7 he had reached Limestone, and by July 25 the goods had arrived in Lexington and the store of "Abijah & John W. Hunt" was open for business.

On July 25, 1795, the *Kentucky Gazette* carried a new advertisement—upside down to attract attention. The only one so printed in this issue, the notice announced that "A. & J. W. Hunt" had opened a store on Main Street opposite the courthouse, in the building "lately occupied by Stephen Collins as a tavern." The proprietors had for sale "a Large and Extensive Assortment of Merchandize, Suited to the present season, as well as Iron Mongery and Books; which they flatter themselves from the terms they were laid in at in Philadelphia, they are enabled to sell as low as any others in this place, by wholesale or retail."

Business was brisk—by mid-October Hunt had returned to Philadelphia to purchase another stock of goods. He dealt with over twenty wholesale firms and once more the largest purchase was from Wilson Hunt. The goods were loaded on the wagons of nine wagoners who contracted to deliver them to James Wilkins, forwarding agent, in Pittsburgh for $6.50 per hundredweight. On December 19 the merchandise had arrived in Lexington and was advertised for sale: "A Large and General Assortment of merchandise, calculated for the present and ensuing season. Also an Extensive Assortment of Iron Mongery, Cutlery, Glass, Queen's Ware [a glazed English Earthenware], Books, and Groceries."

Prices at the Hunt store were competitive. In general the markup was 75 to 100 percent, a figure prevailing in the Midwest. John asked for his brother's opinion on profit-making and Abraham, Jr., replied: "I do not doubt that taking goods to Kentucky is occasioned with a great deal hard labor, Trouble & Anxiety & a Person ought to get well paid for it."

Abraham, Jr., was correct; the physical hazards, transportation costs, and risk justified significant profit. Often the construction of flatboats at Pittsburgh was delayed.

Trunks and barrels sometimes broke apart, spilling the contents. A boat might leak, allowing some items to be soaked. There was always the danger that a boat would hit a snag or sandbar and sink. In 1798 a boatload of salt belonging to the Hunts sank in the Ohio River and "every particle of Salt" was lost. Most merchants of the day probably felt the disgust expressed by one in his journal as he wagoned his goods to Pittsburgh: "I have had a drary time out and am trewly sick of the voyage as well as sick and worn out with this Long fatigueing Journey."

During his first three years in Lexington (1795–1798), John carried on significant trade with the Hunts of Cincinnati. With a population of less than 500 in 1795, Cincinnati was unable to supply sufficient quantities of pork, beef, whiskey, salt, tobacco, and horses to meet the demands of the army and immigrants settling in the Northwest. The town traded extensively with the adjacent area in Northern Kentucky. Although the founders of Cincinnati had dreamed of trade with the Bluegrass region, the roads were too bad and the Licking River unnavigable beyond Falmouth; any major trading between the two areas would have to wait until the railway era.

Early historians do mention, however, that Lexington supplied cattle and nails to Cincinnati, but no documentary evidence has been discovered that merchants other than the Hunts carried on full-scale trading between the two towns. With the Hunts, cattle and a multitude of supplies did indeed head to Cincinnati—but nails passed in the opposite direction, to Lexington.

The Hunt's Lexington-Cincinnati trade centered about army supply for Fort Washington. Abijah frequently visited the advanced posts, became thoroughly familiar with army needs, and developed a reputation of dependability. In November of 1795 he was greeted as the first American merchant to appear at Fort Defiance on the Maumee River. For the year 1796 the government appointed Abijah "grand sutler" or chief contractor for the army in the Northwest and gave him authority to contract with merchants for supplies.

Detailed accounts give a clear and complete view of the Lexington-Cincinnati trade conducted by the Hunts. One product much in demand by the army was liquor. It is well-known that the army had a great thirst at the time. William Henry Harrison came to Fort Washington in 1791 as a young lieutenant and was shocked at the amount of drinking. Supplying the army in the Southwest in 1799, Abijah wrote that he could not get enough whiskey, "as the Consumption is Monstrous in the Army."

Along with liquor, bacon stands out as a Lexington product in demand. In August 1795 John sold 98 gallons of sherry, a barrel of brandy, and 433 pounds of bacon to Cincinnati. On February 1, 1797, John shipped 105½ gallons of peach brandy and 133¼ gallons of whiskey to Jeremiah and Abijah. Butter, cheese, salt, tobacco, horses, and writing paper were sent to Cincinnati. In January 1796 Abijah ordered 100 head of hogs, 50 of beef cattle, and a Negro woman to serve as housekeeper for Major Thomas Dayal. He told John to have the slave bound for twenty years and then freed, since slavery was illegal north of the Ohio; and he suggested that John might send a man and woman so they would be contented.

In return, the Cincinnati Hunts sent John leather from their tannery, shoes, nails, and bills of exchange on the Secretary of War. Leather shipments began in January 1796, with four dozen bridles and several sides of leather. In November 1796 the Cincinnati firm shipped 100 sides of sole leather, 30 sides of upper leather, 2 casks of nails, 120 pairs of shoes, and 4 sheepskins. When the water was high enough for transportation on the Kentucky River, these goods were shipped via Frankfort, which was nearer than Limestone to Lexington. Otherwise they were sent via Limestone. The bridles, shoes, and nails were probably retailed by John, and the leather was probably sold or bartered to Lexington shoemakers.

The two firms were not acting as commission merchants for each other; the goods were sold at wholesale prices when transferred. During the period between August 1795 and September 1797 the total balance in John's favor was £6,438. One thousand pounds of this was in the form of cash paid by John in a purchase of lands for Jeremiah and Abijah. Several other relatively small entries record cash paid out by John for Jeremiah and Abijah. But most of the balance of £6,438 resulted from shipments of produce to Cincinnati. The products sent to Lexington in return did not begin to pay this balance, so the Cincinnati Hunts made up the difference in cash and bills of exchange. For example, on September 12, 1795, John received £1,695 in cash and bills of exchange. On July 6, 1796, he received £900 in bills of exchange on the Secretary of War. Therefore, for the firm of Abijah and John W. Hunt, the Lexington-Cincinnati commerce provided an arrangement for the exchange of produce for much-needed funds.

By supplying the army, Abijah was attempting to solve one of the constant problems of western merchants—the handling of remittances to the East. Goods were obtained in the Atlantic states on credit and sold for cash or bartered for produce in the West. Frontier farmers lacked sufficient cash for necessary purchases so they bartered with the merchants. (Even if pioneer merchants had taken in enough specie to pay their eastern bills, transferring it would have been hazardous and risky.) Transportation difficulties made it difficult for merchants to ship the farm produce they had accepted in payment eastward across the mountains or up the Ohio River. Eventually the Hunts would transport produce to New Orleans, selling it for bills of exchange which were used to pay their debts in Philadelphia. But before 1798 Abijah and his partners supplied the army with provisions and specie and in return, the army pay-master and quartermaster gave them bills of exchange drawn on the Secretary of War. These bills could be sent east safely and were readily accepted by all businessmen. The amount of capital involved was sizable. In February 1796 Abijah sent Wilson Hunt $10,000 drawn on the federal government. During 1797 the Hunts received at least $5,000 in bills of exchange on the Secretary of War. In 1798, when the army transferred to the Southwest, the trade terminated. This was in spite of the fact that Abijah's brothers, Jesse and Jeremiah, continued as prominent businessmen in Cincinnati for many years. It would seem that the trade would have continued if it had involved much more than army supply.

The Hunts accelerated the early commercial development of central Kentucky. In 1796 and 1797 they expanded operations by opening branch stores in Danville, Frankfort, and Shelbyville. Merchandise was shipped from the central store in Lexington to the branches and periodic remittances were made in cash and produce. With this network the Hunt firm served central Kentucky farmers by providing Philadelphia goods and marketing farm products. In the fall of 1796 Abijah and John advertised: "A. & J. W. Hunt, Will Purchase Tobacco of the present year's growth, at their stores in Lexington, Danville, and Frankfort." James Edwards, manager of the branch in Danville, took salt and brandy in barter, and Elijah Smith in Shelbyville received pork for goods. Daniel Weisiger, a well-known tavernkeeper, operated the Hunt store in Frankfort during 1796. At the same time Weisiger acted as forwarding agent, forwarding products of the Hunt's Cincinnati-Lexington trade via the Kentucky River.

In the summer of 1796 rumors of peace in Europe caused a temporary business slump and falling prices. The Hunts, unable to pay all their bills, received many duns late in the year from Philadelphia firms. Abijah reported from Philadelphia in December 1796 that no Kentucky merchants had paid up and the Hunt firms were "equal to the best." He wrote that business was distressed also in Philadelphia, where several respected houses were unable to pay their notes and a number were about to fail. They were consequently sending young men to collect money owed them in Kentucky, and that, Abijah warned, would weed out Lexington's merchants. Although the Hunt credit was still good, great exertion would be necessary to preserve it. He instructed John to sell all the land he could as long as it would bring its value.

John's family in Trenton eagerly read the infrequent letters from Lexington. "We received your letter, my dear John, by Peter Vorhees," his stepmother sighed. "It was extreemly welcome to us all. It was handed from Father to Son & Mother to daughter." John inquired especially about the latest engagements, weddings, births, and deaths. Philemon once gave him this news: "There is great confusion in the family of Mr. Bingham, whose daughter eloped the night before last from her father's house with a French Nobleman, Count de Lilly; they were found next morning at Miss Jones's, a milliner's, & it is said that the lady, who is no more than fifteen, is now locked up by her father. What makes it more disagreeable is the advanced age of the Gentleman, who is about thirty five."

In 1796 a carriage wreck was the subject of family correspondence. John's stepmother, his sister Theodosia, Nancy Higbee (Theodosia's friend), and Lydia (a servant) set out for Cranbury, New Jersey, in a carriage. When Aaron, the family servant who was driving, stopped in Maidenhead to water the horses, the women kept their places. Aaron very imprudently removed the bits from the horses' mouths; they took fright and bolted. The carriage overturned, breaking the body and ripping off the top. Fortunately the horses became entangled in the harness and were unable to drag the carriage. The ladies were all badly shaken up and bruised but no bones were broken. Aaron was trampled but not severely injured by the frightened horses. John's brother informed him that the horses had been worked all summer and were usually very gentle.

When he was twenty-three and ready to marry, John's sister and brothers assisted in the search for a wife. "I was at Philadelphia about three weeks ago," wrote Robert, "where I heard a great many inquiries after your health & some of the Ladies at Mrs. Fullerton's said if you would return with a Baggage Waggon they would visit Kentucky this Spring. . . . Maria &c. are still on hand without any new Beaux so if you have a mind for any of them let me know & they all have such a regard for you I'll undertake to engage any of them." Sister Theodosia was equally encouraging: "Hardly any lady's of your acquaintance are married or going to be so you may come and make a choice. There are some very pretty young girls just grown up." But there were young ladies available nearer at hand.

The household of Colonel Thomas Hart, Lexington's most prominent merchant, seemed to attract young bachelors. Colonel Hart had migrated to Lexington in 1794 from Hagerstown, Maryland, where Thomas Hart, Jr., had married Eleanor Grosh. Eleanor's sisters, Catherine and Sophia, were orphans so she brought them to Kentucky to live with her. The Grosh family had emigrated to Maryland from Germany in 1746, and the three sisters were first cousins of Francis Scott Key, who was to be the author of "The Star Spangled Banner." In addition to the Grosh sisters, the Hart family included two unmarried daughters of the Colonel—Nancy and Lucretia Hart. Nancy married the lawyer and future statesman and diplomat, James Brown. Lucretia became the wife of Henry Clay. Sophia Grosh married Henry's brother, Porter Clay, and Catherine Grosh won John's heart.

Nineteen years old in 1796, Catherine was beautiful. Almost as tall as John, she was slim and graceful with warm deep blue eyes, slender little mouth, loosely curled dark brown hair, and feminine neck. She had a kind, friendly expression and was more open and outgoing than John. She shared his taste for music, drama, parties, and church work. Like him, she approached life seriously and required neatness and order.

In September 1797 John proudly took Catherine to be his wife. He was twenty-five and she was twenty. Sister Theodosia responded to the news: "I take this opportunity my dear brother of congratulating you on your marriage and of telling you how much we all wish to see and love our new sister." Later she observed: "We have heard our new sister is very handsome and accomplished, that she plays on the Piano. How I wish to hear her! You must, indeed you must bring her here this fall. But the sweet disposition you tell me she possesses will be of far greater consequence to your happiness than either beauty or accomplishments."

During his first two years of marriage John's business career was once more affected by the war between England and France. The French government, claiming that the United States had betrayed France with the Jay Treaty, resumed the seizure of American vessels in the summer of 1796. Diplomatic relations between France and the United States deteriorated into the quasi war of 1798 and 1799. Captures of American merchant vessels raised insurance rates and caused insecurity in the commodity import trade. American businessmen, also alarmed at the report in April 1797 of the suspension of specie payments by the Bank of England, found the years 1797 and 1798 a time of declining prices and unsettled, depressed conditions.

Abijah informed John in April 1797 that business in the East was stagnant and property values were falling because of the threat of war with France. He believed that John should do only "snug business," that is, that

32

he should sell goods only for cash and refrain from investing in uncertain speculations. John should also sell the lands belonging to the firm and do all he could to collect outstanding debts. By the spring of 1798 they had paid substantially all of their more than four-thousand-pound account with Meeker, Cochran & Company of Philadelphia, but they were still behind on other payments and remained so as long as their partnership continued. One result of the business slump was that by the fall of 1798 the Hunts discontinued operation of the branch stores.

A portion of the funds used to pay the eastern debts was obtained from the shipment of produce to New Orleans. Western merchants and producers floated tobacco, flour, whiskey, and other products down the Ohio and Mississippi on flatboats to Natchez or New Orleans. There they were sold to Spanish inhabitants of western Florida and Louisiana, exported to the West Indies and southern Europe, or shipped to the eastern United States. The river trade provided the most feasible outlet for western goods, and without it western farmers would have had little incentive to produce above the subsistence level.

The Hunts were not the first entrepreneurs to develop the New Orleans market. James Wilkinson had initially opened the trade in 1787. The Hunts probably would have exported down the Mississippi River earlier if they had not opened the Cincinnati trade and engaged in supplying the army there. For them the boating of produce to New Orleans replaced the Cincinnati trade in furnishing money which could be used to make remittances to the East. When the Hunts embarked upon the river trade in 1798, western exports down the Mississippi were rapidly increasing.

The first shipment by Hunt consisted of thirty-eight hogsheads of tobacco loaded on a flatboat in the Kentucky River at Frankfort on March 21, 1798. By April 8 a second boat under John Masterson was drifting downstream with another forty-six hogsheads. John W. Hunt wrote to Lanthois, Pitot & Company, commission and forwarding merchants in New Orleans, giving very clear and concise instructions on how to handle the shipments. They were to sell the tobacco in New Orleans if it would bring eight dollars per hundredweight. If it would not, they were to purchase insurance and send the cargo to Pearson Hunt in Philadelphia. If no vessel bound for that port was available, they were to send the tobacco to Baltimore or to New York and, if possible, they were to divide the cargo, putting it on different ships to lessen the risk. If the tobacco could not be sold soon, they were to make an advance to Hunt's boatmen for their pay and expenses on the trip back to Kentucky.

The first boat had arrived and its cargo had been sold by May 23. Inspection at the expense of the purchaser revealed that "every hogshead had got Wet by the head up in the flat," and some of the tobacco in each was spoiled. The damaged tobacco was repacked separately, leaving thirty-six undamaged hogsheads of the thirty-eight on the first boat. The account of sale received by Hunt, interesting in its use of dollars and bits (eighths of a dollar) instead of dollars and cents, appears opposite.

Hunt's minimum price could not be obtained for the second shipment; and, since all the ships in the harbor operated under Spanish permits, it could not be shipped to the Atlantic states without paying a duty of 21 percent. Many ships were expected but "from the War so much Spoken of, between france and the United States," Hunt's agents in New Orleans feared they would be unable to ship his tobacco. They sold the flatboats, paid Masterson $180, Hart $250, and allowed the crews to leave for Kentucky before the second shipment was sold. On June 21 John Lanthois requested permission to sell the second forty-six hogsheads for seven dollars per hundred, but on July 9 he was able to sell for eight dollars. The damaged tobacco from the first ship-

1798   Acct. Sale and net. proceed of thirty Six
        hogsheads of tobacco received of Messrs.
        A & Jhn. Wm. Hunt and sold for their ac-
        count.

Viz.

May 23   36 hogsheads of tobacco sold to Fortier &
          Prillet, net 37340 lb. at $8 per %   2987.1½

Charges

To the Intendant's Secretary	4.	
Negroes hire to unload	6.4	
Cartage	8.6½	
Storage for a month	9.	
Duties	74.6½	
Negroes hire to Sell	5.	
Comm. on $2987.1½	149.3	

255.4

Net Proceed $2731.5½

E. E. New Orleans the 27th of May 1798

Lanthois Pitot & Co.

ment was also sold, and in July the company remitted
John Hunt $3,414 and two bits.

In 1798 Abijah moved to Natchez. Probably the main
reason was the shift in army strength from the Northwest to the Southwest. The army was pushing into the
area north of the thirty-first parallel, claimed by the
United States since 1783 but occupied by Spain until
after Pinckney's Treaty in 1795. Commanding General
James Wilkinson established Fort Adams south of Natchez in the fall of 1798, and in March 1799 the army replaced Spanish troops in Natchez. Abijah was in the
Mississippi Territory by December 1798, when he was
involved in a $400-purchase of blankets and supplies for
the Indians. Abijah continued furnishing whiskey and
other provisions and specie to the army as he had done
in the Northwest. In March 1799 he acquired $12,000 in

bills on the Secretary of War and $7,000 on the quarter-master general at Pittsburgh. In the summer of 1800 he obtained a receipt of $18,525 signed by the paymaster of the Third Regiment for money which he had furnished for "pay, forage & Subsistance for the troops Garrisoned at Fort Adams & Fort Stoddart up to Feb. 28, 1800."

In the spring of 1799 John Hunt shipped a load of produce to Abijah in Natchez. John commissioned Jacob Curtner to take a boat from Frankfort to Natchez and New Orleans. The boat was laden with twenty-five hogsheads of tobacco and a quantity of flour, hats, nails, bacon, whiskey, soap, and butter. He instructed Curtner to proceed to "Col. Taylors [probably Zachary Taylor's father, Colonel Richard Taylor] who lives about two miles from the mouth of Goose Creek this side of the Falls of the Ohio" and join another merchant's boat for the trip to Natchez. Along the river during the trip, Curtner was to sell what produce he could at prices specified by John. At Natchez he was supposed to deliver everything except the tobacco to Abijah, unless Abijah decided certain products would sell better in New Orleans. The tobacco was consigned to Nicholas Ridgely in New Orleans.

Hunt wrote Ridgely to inform him that the tobacco was consigned to his house, directing him to sell it in New Orleans or forward it to Pearson Hunt in Philadelphia. Hunt expected $6.50 per hundred but left it up to Ridgely to decide whether to sell or ship it. "You may undertake to recommed it as being the Best Tobacco Shiped from this country," Hunt wrote. If sale was expected soon, Ridgely was to detain Curtner so that Curtner could bring the remittance to Lexington. Hunt instructed Ridgely to pay from $300 to $350 to Curtner for paying his hands and expenses on the trip home.

The tobacco was sold and Curtner and crew returned safely to Kentucky. Such was not the case for an agent of Abijah's at this time. Robert McCrea and four companions rode out of Natchez on March 4, 1799, heading northeast on the Natchez Trace. McCrea's saddlebags contained one packet of papers addressed to John W. Hunt, another to Jesse Hunt in Cincinnati, and two from General Wilkinson in Natchez to the Secretary of War. As far as McCrea knew the papers included $20,000 in bills of exchange from Abijah Hunt. Actually the amount was $25,000. The five men also carried over $1,000 in cash of their own. On March 19, at about midnight, they were asleep in their camp near the Tennessee River when five armed Indians—or white men dressed as Indians—fell upon them. Two men escaped, but McCrea and the others were tied to trees and robbed of all they had, including the horses. After the thieves left, McCrea and party found a canoe drifting on the Tennessee River and floated down to Fort Massac where they immediately sent word to Abijah Hunt by a boat heading toward New Orleans. When McCrea arrived in Cincinnati a few days later, letters were mailed to several people in Philadelphia requesting that payment be stopped on the bills. Payment was stopped, duplicate bills were sent, and the only inconvenience to John and Abijah was the delay involved.

In 1800 and 1801 John cooperated with Abijah, Jeremiah, and Jesse Hunt in exporting Kentucky slaves to Mississippi. They were among the first to send slaves to the Southwest, in a trade which was to continue until the Civil War. In reporting New Orleans prices and market demands during this period, Abijah always stressed that Negroes sold better than anything else and commanded cash. In the autumn of 1800 he sent $3,000 to Jeremiah and requested that he and John begin purchasing slaves. The Hunts approached several potential sellers in Kentucky. John Adair of Mercer County, an Indian fighter and future governor of Kentucky, first declined to sell. Then on December 19, Adair changed his mind and agreed to part with four men, four women, and four children, "all very likely, two of the women are big with child. two of the men are under bad characters.

One is a tolerable good Carpenter, one a Hatter, & one as good a Distiller & powdermaker as any. They are really sealable & I believe will now go down the river willingly. I have told them they are to go, & they promise perfect obedience, they are at liberty to run if they choose." Adair agreed to sell the twelve for 1,000 pounds.

At John's request Jeremiah called on Joseph Mosby and purchased fourteen-year-old Mary for shipment on John's account. She was the only slave Mosby would part with because the others were in families. Mary was purchased for $233.33, which was as cheap as any slave purchase Jeremiah had made for cash. Mary was given new clothing and transported to Natchez on a boat commanded by Philip Buckner, land speculator and founder of Augusta, Kentucky.

While the export of slaves to the Southwest was a new kind of venture, it was no innovation for Kentucky merchants to engage in land speculation. Abijah and John Hunt were involved in the practice to a moderate degree. In 1796 they paid state taxes on 4,652 acres of land in Kentucky. Experiencing difficulty in paying their debts in the East, they began selling land that year. In July they advertised to sell 1,500 acres and half interest in a ferry on the Licking River at Cynthiana. Their advertisement stated: "We will sell the above property *Very Low*, as we are in want of money, and will give a good and sufficient title." In December an additional 1,000-acre tract was advertised. Fayette County deed books reveal that from December 1796 through May 1797 they sold a total of 6,438 acres; but there appears to be no true indication of the price. The Hunt partners were taxed for 1,714 acres in 1797, and for only 900 in 1800. On his own account, John held 500 acres in 1800 in addition to several town lots, the latter with a combined value of $200; in 1801 he held 3,392 acres, and in 1802 this figure had risen to 3,892 acres. He clearly made a profit on a 500-acre tract in Green County purchased for $1,000 in 1799 and sold for $1,300 in 1805.

In the summer of 1800 the partnership between Abijah and John was terminated by mutual consent. Since 1798, when the original three-year term ended, John had been considering a break with Abijah. He complained to his brother Wilson that he did all the work for the house but received only half the profits. This was basically true, but John had used Abijah's capital and connections. The dissolution was amicable, and the partners continued to cooperate in business ventures for several years. The fact that John traveled to Philadelphia to purchase goods at the time of the dissolution indicates that he planned to continue in merchandising for the moment at least.

It is not certain exactly how much longer John did maintain the mercantile business, but before mid-February of 1801 he had sold his merchandise, had bought a 500-acre farm in Fayette County, and had begun farming. He continued to collect debts due the store in order to pay its creditors in the East. In August 1801 he told his father that he was nearly out of debt. The Natchez and New Orleans trade had brought in sufficient funds to reduce the accounts substantially. It is difficult to determine exactly what John's financial state was in 1801. Individuals and firms to whom he had extended credit still owed him money. A settlement with Abijah had not been made, and Abijah was indebted to John. Tax records clearly indicate that he was solvent. In 1801 John paid state taxes on 500 acres of land in Fayette County, 3,392 acres in other Kentucky counties, two Lexington town lots valued at $300, lots in Washington, Kentucky, valued at $1,000, eleven slaves, and four horses.

During his first six years in Lexington, Hunt had helped to accelerate the westward movement. He had transported large quantities of manufactured goods from Philadelphia and sold them at retail to the troops of the Northwest and to frontiersmen in Cincinnati and in central Kentucky. He had traded Lexington products for goods produced in Cincinnati. With his cousins he had marketed Kentucky farm products and slaves in New Orleans and Natchez and he had speculated in land. Hunt and other entrepreneurs had opened and developed the commerce of the Ohio Valley.

Rising merchants in the United States in the late eighteenth and early nineteenth centuries often invested accumulated capital in manufacturing. Entrepreneurs such as Hunt were usually on the lookout for new ventures which appeared profitable. By 1801 the business slump of the previous three years had caused John to become discouraged with merchandising. His credit was excellent, and he had a good reputation and connections from Philadelphia to New Orleans. He decided to invest his time, energy, and capital in horse breeding and in the manufacture of hemp products.

4

RACEHORSES

During the years of the partnership with Abijah the people of Lexington learned to trust and respect John W. Hunt. In the winter of 1797 when one of his friends had to be out of town, he depended on John to care for his daughter, providing her proper clothing and a place to stay. In December 1798 Hunt was appointed postmaster. The first postmaster, Innes B. Brent, who was also county jailer, had been keeping the box holding the mail on the mantel above the fireplace in the public room of the log jail. Hunt moved the post office to Postlethwaite's Tavern and then, in 1801, to the office of the *Kentucky Gazette.*

Postmasters were appointed for no specific term and held office at the pleasure of the postmaster general. When, in 1801, the Republicans under Thomas Jefferson replaced the Federalists in control of the national government, postmasters such as Hunt were in a vulnerable position. Postmaster General Joseph Habersham was replaced by Republican Gideon Granger in 1801, and in May 1802 Granger notified Hunt that he was to be replaced by John Jordan. No evidence has been found that Hunt had Federalist sympathies. He may have been removed because he was less of a Republican than Jordan, or perhaps because the Republicans hoped to win a friend by appointing a new man. It is certain that Hunt did not resign and that he was not removed for malfeasance. The General Post Office assured him: "There is no doubt but that you have executed the duties of your office faithfully."

Shortly after his appointment as postmaster Catherine presented John with their first child, a daughter, whom they named Mary. "The family all join with me," said Philemon, "in expressions of love to Mrs. Hunt & to your little daughter, whom we are told, you cannot suffer to be out of your arms." The next year, during his trip to Philadelphia and Trenton, he acquired a puppy for his one-year-old. The new family treated visitors with hospitality. A Philadelphia businessman expressed appreciation: "Sir, I have left a box of *merchandize,* to be forwarded to you by the first opportunity. Also a keg containing some cherries. . . . With thanks to you & your amiable consort, for your attention, when in your country."

During this same period John's brothers in the East were attempting to establish careers. At the age of twenty, in 1798, Robert was graduated from Princeton and finished his clerkship in law. He had to wait a year until he was twenty-one before he could enter practice, and by that time he had apparently contracted tuberculosis. He recovered long enough to serve for a few months as captain of infantry in the fall of 1799. For nearly two years he attempted to practice law, but each time he went to court he found he was too weak. He caught colds easily, especially when he changed his routine. However, in 1800 John read: "Robert is rather better. His cough continues and whether it will ever wane away seems to be uncertain."

Young Abraham, Jr., was apprenticed to his father, but before he could accomplish his goal of entering the dry goods business he became consumptive in 1798 and died "with uncommon resignation" in less than a year. Youngest brother Philemon, the honor student at Princeton, never completed his education. In 1800 his father reported: "Philemon has for some time been Lame, in the calves of his Legs. He has scarce any pain when he is in Bed or when up sitting still, but he can walk only with difficulty. He is strangely afflicted & without knowing the cause." His father soon became fearful that he would waste away as it appeared to be "a decay." Less than six months after John first learned of Philemon's illness, he received word that "Poor Philemon has at last fallen, a victim to his love for study and the confined life he led at Princeton." Having served as an officer in the navy during the quasi war with France, Theodore sailed to China on a merchantman in 1801. Wilson and Pearson continued separate wholesale businesses in Philadelphia.

One thing John held in common with his fellow Kentuckians was a fervent interest in fine horses. The Virginians and Carolinians who settled the Bluegrass region brought their horses with them and found the climate and pastures in the limestone areas quite favorable for the development of thoroughbreds. From Lexington's earliest days horse racing was one of the major amusements. In 1787 the trustees of the town halted racing on the "Commons" (the banks of the Town Branch). Advertisements for thoroughbreds standing for service in 1787 and 1788 indicate that horsemen were already attempting to improve bloodlines. In 1789 the *Kentucky Gazette* announced the running of a purse race, and there has been racing in Lexington on a regular basis ever since.

During the two decades after the American Revolution, interest in racing intensified throughout the nation. In the colonial period English thoroughbred horses had been imported into Virginia, Maryland, and South Carolina. After 1783 importations increased, and new racing stables were established in New York, New Jersey, and other Atlantic states. Jockey clubs were formed to build racecourses and to regulate racing. The crowds at the tracks became larger and included a wider range of social classes than previously. A number of English stallions were transferred to Kentucky and Tennessee after standing as studs for several seasons in the eastern states.

In Lexington a jockey club was organized in the fall of 1797. From 1787 to about 1812, there were several advertisements every spring for thoroughbreds standing for stud service in Lexington. Most of them were either imported English horses or their descendants. About 1812 interest declined, but breeding and training as well as racing continued. In 1828 a fine new racecourse was constructed, and the Lexington races became the most important in the West.

As we have seen, John W. Hunt's father and grandfather had been interested in the breeding of fine turf horses, or running horses. An excellent horseman himself, John enjoyed working with horses and attending races, but apparently he had little direct involvement in racing. In November 1802, at the age of thirty, he brought his entrepreneurial energies to the Kentucky horse industry. He asked his father in Trenton to look for a turf horse that would be a good covering horse (stud) to bring to Kentucky from the East. The following year John entered into partnership with Ralph Phillips, a long-time family friend from Maidenhead, New Jersey. The two men had agreed to an equal partnership, sharing jointly in both expenses and profits. Phillips purchased several of the best imported horses in the East and arranged for their delivery to Hunt in Lexington.

The greatest risk in the business was the arduous journey across the mountains. In general the imported stallions brought to Kentucky and Tennessee were advanced in age. Covering fees were higher in the East, so young thoroughbreds recently imported were first placed for stud service in the Atlantic states. As the demand for a stallion's service decreased and as he grew older, his value declined to the point that westerners could expect to profit by purchasing him. But the buyer had to be careful to acquire horses which would survive the western trip. If the horse arrived in Kentucky or Tennessee in good condition, there was the less risk that he would die prematurely.

One of the first two horses Phillips and Hunt brought to Lexington died almost as soon as he arrived. Baronet was a bay horse, foaled in England in 1785 and imported into New York in 1791 or 1792. On October 29, 1803, Phillips, as Hunt's partner, purchased him in New York from John Jacob Astor's brother Henry for $2,000. Phillips had reservations about sending him. He consulted Hunt's father in Trenton and asked whether he should send Baronet or another imported horse named Royalist. Abraham Hunt preferred Baronet because he believed him a finer horse and because Royalist seemed vicious and dangerous to handle. Early in November of 1803 Phillips placed Baronet and another horse named Paymaster in the care of a groom who was to lead the stallions to Lexington.

Meanwhile Hunt prepared for the arrival of the horses. On October 25, 1803, he advertised that "the celebrated, full bred Imported Horse *Baronet,*" was on his way from New York to Lexington. "He has perhaps won more money than any other horse ever imported from England; he won at one time the Oatland Stakes of 1900 Guineas, beating 18 of the best horses in the kingdom of Great Britain." At some time late in 1803 or early the next year, Baronet and Paymaster arrived; by April 29, 1804, Baronet was dead. It is doubtful that he served a single mare in Lexington. Hunt's half interest in Baronet—$1,000—was of course totally lost. Abraham Hunt, regretting that he had chosen Baronet over Royalist, paid Phillips $500 on John's account.

Paymaster did not make up for the loss. His distinguished pedigree notwithstanding, Kentuckians disapproved of Paymaster. It may be that at sixteen hands and rising he was too large to suit Kentucky preferences. After two years Hunt returned him to the East where his services were appreciated.

Baronet had died and Paymaster had been a disappointment. But the third horse brought to Lexington by Hunt and Phillips was a decided success. Royalist was sent to take the place of Baronet alongside Paymaster in Hunt's stable in the spring of 1804. John's advertisement reveals his pride in the acquisition:

The Celebrated Imported, and Real

bred Turf Horse.

Royalist,

Has arrived from New-York and will stand this season at the same stable with Paymaster, in this place. . . .

Royalist is a full blooded racer; he was bred by his royal highness the Prince of Wales [later King George IV] & sold to Thomas Bullock esq. who kept him as a racer until he was purchased by Mr. Abraham Skinner, who imported him in the ship James, from England to New York. He is a beautiful bay, handsomely marked, with a star and snip, 15 hands 3 inches high, well proportioned, fine action, free from all blemishes, and while in England, performed equal to any horse of his age. . . .

PERFORMANCES.

In 1793, at three years old, the first time he started, he won 400 guineas at New-Market, beating Lord Grosvenor's chestnut Filly, by Pot8o's, out of Mariane, and the Duke of Bedford's colt by High-flyer, out of Conegonde. He started for the Craven stakes, and beat Dare Devil, Agamemnon, Coriander, Seagull, Golden Rod, Fort William and six others. . . .

PEDIGREE.

This is to certify, that the bay horse Royalist . . . was got by Saltram, son of Eclipse; his dam by Herod; his grand dam, by Marik; great grand dam by Blank; great great grand dam by Driver; great, great, great grand dam by Smiling Tom; great,

46

great, great, great grand dam by Oysterfoot; great, great, great, great, great, grand dam by Commoner; great, great, great, great, great, great, grand dam the Duke of Summerset's Copper Mare.

This is a true pedigree,

(Signed)   Thomas Bullock.
London, March 31, 1796.

Royalist's pedigree was equal to that of any stallion in Lexington, and his covering fee was equal to the highest. The price was thirty dollars for the season and forty dollars to guarantee a foal. Royalist stood in Lexington during 1804 and 1805. The year 1805 appears to have been a heyday in the breeding of racehorses in the Bluegrass region. Two horses had papers equal to Royalist's—Stirling and Spread Eagle (both thirty dollars the season). Speculator brought twenty-four dollars for the season, and Young Baronet, Forrester, Nimrod, Lamp-lighter, and Albert were available for somewhat smaller fees.

Royalist attracted the attention of western horsemen from as far away as Nashville. In the summer of 1805, William P. Anderson of that city sent two mares to be bred to Royalist and expressed an interest in buying him. William and his brother Patton, friends and business associates of Andrew Jackson, had begun construction of a racetrack in the spring of 1805 near the mercantile establishment belonging to Jackson and John Hutchings. The site was three miles from the Hermitage and eight miles from Nashville. And that year Jackson and Hutchings took over two-thirds interest in the course and enlarged and improved it.

In June 1805 Anderson wrote to Hunt that he and his family planned to visit the Hunt family and that he hoped to "be able to *Cousin* you out of him (or some other one equally as good) to stand the next season in this place. . . . Indeed the very name of *royalist* sounds grand in my ears." By autumn the visit had not been made but Anderson was still interested. He informed Hunt that he and Andrew Jackson were also eager to bring Hunt's "fine running mare" to Nashville for racing on their new racecourse. This is the only reference we have found to indicate Hunt himself raced horses. There is no record of the sale of the mare, but in early 1806 Hunt agreed to the sale of half of Royalist to Anderson. It has not been possible to determine the terms. Accounts indicate that Anderson turned over $700 worth of cotton to Hunt's commercial agent in Nashville early in 1807.

Advertising in the Nashville newspapers that Royalist was on his way, Anderson had handbills printed. He was jubilant that Royalist's opposition as a first-rate covering horse would be greatly reduced; Andrew Jackson's Truxton and Joseph Erwin's Ploughboy would be unavailable for covering service because they were training for a race to be held on April 3, 1806. Anderson stated that Jackson would do all he could to further the career of Royalist in Tennessee. Less than two months after the sale was closed, Anderson reported that Royalist was making "a very great season." In July he told Hunt that the horse had covered 140 mares during the spring season—a great season indeed! Before the year ended Hunt sold his half of Royalist to Anderson and his associates in Tennessee. Undoubtedly, Royalist had been a profitable investment for Hunt. After his two successful years in Lexington, the horse must have sold for a considerable sum.

In the spring of 1805, while Paymaster stood somewhere in Kentucky and Royalist was in Lexington, a third imported thoroughbred belonging to Hunt and Phillips was having a good season in Jefferson County, Kentucky. Blossom, foaled in England in 1795, had covered seventy mares before the end of May. Hunt made plans to place Blossom in Paris, Kentucky, for the following year.

Thoroughbred stallion owners always attempted to establish the reputation of their horses as sure foal-getters. If a horse failed to produce a high percentage of foals, mare owners would not use him. John and others published testimonials from horsemen to the effect that the horse in question was known to be productive. On the other hand, in 1805 Hunt and Phillips possessed, on joint account, a thoroughbred who definitely was a poor procreator. It was fortunate that Phillips learned that the horse named Highflyer was not a sure foal-getter. If the horse had been sent to Kentucky, he would have damaged Hunt's reputation as a breeder. Instead Phillips placed him with Isaac and Gilbert D. Lowe, tavern-keepers in Lancaster, Pennsylvania. Phillips informed the Lowes that Highflyer was not productive but he did not want the fact to become known in the area. Nevertheless, the word got around. The result was that in 1805 Highflyer covered only twelve mares. By November Phillips had traded him for the thoroughbred Badger.

Ralph Phillips had contact with some of the best horsemen in New Jersey, Pennsylvania, and New York, but Hunt came to desire a horse from Virginia. When Phillips did not respond to such requests, Hunt bought one on his own account. In the summer of 1806, Hunt wrote to Wade Hampton, wealthy planter of Columbia, South Carolina, inquiring whether Hampton would sell his valuable imported horse Dragon. Hampton's asking price was $3,000, but Hunt bought the horse in 1806 for $2,500. Dragon was a highly successful investment. He stood in Lexington for four years—1807 through 1810. He had been brought from England by Colonel John Hoomes of Virginia, who was one of the most influential importers of thoroughbreds in the late nineteenth century. A member of the Diomed family (one of the greatest strains in early American racing), Dragon was perhaps Hunt's greatest single contribution to the development of Lexington as a thoroughbred center.

Hunt's advertisement for Dragon follows:

The Celebrated, Imported and Real
Bred Turf Horse,
DRAGON.

This justly celebrated and unequalled horse of horses, whose claim to superiority is not questioned is now in my stable (in high health and good condition) where he stood the two last seasons, and will stand the ensuing under the direction and management of Mr. George Sourbrey jr. . . .

DRAGON is a dark chestnut, handsomely marked, with a star and snip, and without exaggeration is fully sixteen hands high; he is descended from the best running stock in England, and is a brother, in blood, to the famous horse Diomede, whose stock is so highly esteemed in Virginia. It is a fact well known to a number of gentlemen in this state, how desirous the late Col. John Hoomes, of the Bowling Green, Virginia, was to obtain this horse, and never could effect it until after the death of the late Duke of Bedford, who owned him in England. . . .

JOHN W. HUNT.

Lexington, March 26th, 1809.

The advertisement included a statement signed by Wade Hampton which described Dragon's racing career. Dragon had won twenty-two of the most important races in England before the end of his fifth year of racing. His pedigree revealed that he was "got by Woodpecker, one of the best sons of King Herod, his dam June, (who is also the dam of Young Eclipse, and full sister to the dam of Diomed) by Spectator, his grand dam (sister of Horatius) by Blank. . . ." Evidently Hunt kept Dragon in Lexington for several seasons, then sold him to horsemen in Tennessee. Dragon was standing in Nashville in 1811 and died there in 1812.

John displayed the ability to redirect his investments at the right moment when he got out of horse breeding and became a commission merchant in 1810. The horse industry was less profitable by this time. The number of advertisements in the *Kentucky Gazette* decreased from

several in 1811 to one in 1812. Possibly as a consequence of the War of 1812, interest in racing and horse breeding lessened for the time being.

Hunt became widely known as a breeder of cattle, hogs, and mules as well as horses. He liked to boast about a huge sow raised on his farm, and in 1833 an Elizabethtown, Kentucky resident inquired of him: "I have been informed that you are extensively engaged in raising mules and that you can inform me where I can get a Jack of the largest kind and one which has proved himself to be a sure foal getter and is fierce or quick in covering mares."

In the 1840s Hunt was the initiator of the breeding of thoroughbred trotters in Lexington. Until about this time the Bluegrass horsemen had concentrated upon the breeding of running and saddle horses. William T. Porter, editor of *The Spirit of the Times,* a New York magazine of racing and other sports, wrote in 1840 that Kentucky trotters lacked bone and stamina. "They are what would be termed here 'Dandy horses;' they have generally fine heads, and forehanded are well put up but have no more thighs, stifles, and gaskins than a sheep. . . . They go off ten miles pretty well, at the rate of six or seven miles the hour, and then cave in; they are dead beat by a sharp drive of fifteen or twenty miles." By 1840 Kentucky roads had improved and there was a demand for fast road horses. John Hervey, historian of the trotter in America, has written that John W. Hunt was the first to realize the need for development of the trotter in Lexington and the first to attempt to meet it.

In 1839 Hunt asked William T. Porter to act as his agent in the purchase of two of the best trotting stallions in the East. Porter's selections were Abdallah and Commodore, sons of Mambrino, who was the son of Messenger. Porter described Commodore as a "rich blood bay, with no other white than a pretty star, and over sixteen hands high, of immense substance and power. He is a horse of noble presence, and unusually fine action." The horses left New York in February 1840, and were in Lexington for the spring season. Commodore appeared very stylish and showy to the Bluegrass mare owners and he became the most popular light harness covering horse in the Lexington area for many years. John's son Thomas, who shared his love for horses, informed him in 1841: "Commodore is in splendid order and . . . will make a full season. I like his colts very much. They have excellent heads and are very gay." While none of his foals were racers, several of Commodore's daughters became celebrated as broodmares. One produced the stallion, Steven's Bald Chief, the sire of the great trotting broodmare Minnehaha. Minnehaha was the dam of Beautiful Bells and Eva, both of which produced families of champions.

Abdallah, on the other hand, became an object of ridicule in Kentucky. The horse was so ugly and ferocious that many mares and mare owners were repulsed. He had an enormous head, a hollow back, and rat tail. One horseman observed that Abdallah's light middle-piece made him look like "an animal with two fantastic ends joined by an attenuated cylinder." Some observers characterized him as the ugliest horse they ever saw. Abdallah's ferocious temper matched his ugliness. Hunt imported him to Kentucky to sire harness racers; yet Abdallah had not been broken to harness himself. Lexington groom Dennis Seals attempted to break him to harness but the old horse would have none of it and Seals failed.

It is testimony to John's business acumen that he salvaged a profit from the venture. Abdallah stood at the Hunt farm on Leestown Pike about one mile from Lexington. One story relates that he served about fifty mares; another that he produced only eight or ten foals. Two of these were Frank Forester and O'Blennis, the first two 2:30 trotters in history got by the same sire. Abdallah had a good reputation in the East so that after one season Hunt was able to sell him in New York. He had paid $1,000 for Abdallah and sold him for the reputed price of $1,365. Not only had Hunt profited from Commodore and Abdallah, he had also sparked an interest in harness horses which grew rapidly in Lexington during the following years.

Concerning the purchase of Commodore and Abdallah in 1840, *The Spirit of the Times* commented: "Mr. Hunt deserves well of his fellow citizens for his spirit in this matter. He has done much to improve the Cattle and Hogs, etc., in Kentucky, by the importation of several varieties of each, and we are glad he has been induced to extend his operations, as a judicious practical breeder and agriculturist, by the introduction of two capital stallions, from which to breed an improved stock of horses for the ordinary purposes of life."

In advancing the Kentucky horse industry, Hunt contributed to the development of one of the basic sectors of the regional economy. The Bluegrass area continued to breed champion horses and the thoroughbred became a symbol of Kentucky. Generations of carriage owners benefited by Hunt's innovative role in initiating improvement in the trotter or harness horse. Hunt and his partner Phillips brought at least six valuable thoroughbreds to the Bluegrass area. Four of these (Baronet, Paymaster, Royalist, and Blossom) are listed in the national and international bloodline books as having distinguished pedigrees. In addition, he was overseer for the care of three thoroughbreds sent to Kentucky by James Tate of Long Island. On his own he purchased Dragon, one of the finest stallions in the country. Hunt had a part in the transfer to the state of at least two stallions for the breeding of saddle horses for general use. Horses identified with Hunt served mares in Lexington, Danville, Paris, and in Madison and Jefferson counties. At least two, Royalist and Dragon, were taken to Nashville where they contributed to the bloodlines of Tennessee horses.

5

HEMP

At the same time that Hunt was making his contributions to the horse industry, he was becoming at least equally prominent as a manufacturer of hemp. As a merchant he had forwarded the development of Lexington as a commercial city; as a manufacturer he had a key role in making the town a center of the hemp industry. To be near the hemp factory which he established in 1803, John moved his family from the farm to a brick house on the southwest corner of Market and Second streets.

It was exhilarating living in Lexington in the early nineteenth century. Optimism prevailed; the atmosphere of progress produced by the construction of new buildings and the establishment of new institutions was stimulating, almost intoxicating—a city, a cultural center was rising out of the forest. Hunt helped erect a building for the Episcopal church, rented a pew, and supported the organization of a parish. In 1802 he was among the group of citizens who signed a pledge supporting Transylvania University's effort to attract the Reverend James Madison as president. The community leaders pledged to guarantee an annual income of $1,000 to the university for five years if the institution would raise tuition and if Madison accepted the position. (The tuition was raised but Madison, a cousin of

President James Madison, preferred to remain president at William and Mary College.) John and Catherine encouraged the presentation of plays by the students of Transylvania and the Thespian Society. Beginning in 1810 professional acting companies came to town, presenting Macbeth, Othello, and other Shakespearean dramas.

John's pleasure in the busy life of Lexington must have been marred somewhat by the news from the family in Trenton; all too frequently the story was one of trouble and tragedy. Robert, the young lawyer, continued to decline. When he was twenty-four, he told John: "I made another attempt . . . to attend Court and pursue my profession, but I was evidently so much worse after it that, I have now abandoned every idea of the kind and must try to be content myself with an idle life for some time." Less than a year later Robert died.

Returning to the navy for the Tripolitan War (1801–1805), young Theodore was a lieutenant on the *Philadelphia* when it was captured by the Tripolitans in the Mediterranean Sea in October 1803. He was among the prisoners held by the enemy until peace was made between the United States and Tripoli in June 1805. Abraham Hunt accepted this in the same manner as he accepted the other family misfortunes. With quiet resignation he told John that he had written to the naval authorities, that they were doing all they could, and that Theodore's letters revealed he was being treated as well as could be expected. Word came of Theodore's release in September 1805. "This week the blessed news has arrived of peace with Tripoli, and the consequent release of dear Theodore and his companions. In three or four weeks we shall once more be rejoiced by the sight of the dear fellow. He once was the greatest fidget anywhere to be met with. In his last letter he says the room they were confined in, was so small he could not tell whether he continued to be . . . [such a fidget] or not." Theodore left the merchant marine at the outbreak of the War of 1812, when he opened a store in Saint Louis.

John's sister Theodosia, failing to persuade him to move back to New Jersey, pleaded for more frequent visits. "How I wish the accommodations and roads would permit you to pay us a visit," she wrote Catherine. "You cannot imagine how wild I am & how anxious my parents are to see you & the children or you would prevail upon your husband to bring you in this Summer. Those wretched mountains, why do they form such a barrier to the union of families & friends?" Another time in a letter to John she dreamed: "How I wish I could transport myself into your parlour when you, your wife and children are together, take a look at you and fly back." It was heartbreaking when, a year after Robert died, twenty-one-year-old Theodosia became plagued with the same symptoms. For four years she gradually weakened until in December, 1808, she died.

John's own offspring fared better. At thirty he had four children; after Mary had come Theodosia, Charlton, and Eleanor. While he managed stallions and manufactured hemp products during the period before the War of 1812, three more children were born: Henrietta, John Wilson, and Abraham. Worrying about the little Hunts when away, John asked his associates to apprise him of their welfare. "Will thank you to write me once a week," he directed on one trip. Thomas D. Carneal gave this report: "I spent last evening with your family. They are all well. Mary will write by the next mail. Mrs. Hunt the mail after agreeable to arrangement. Wishing you health and a quick return to the bosom of your family." Once when both John and Catherine were away they learned: "Your children are all well. I see them almost every day as I pass, but this morning I went over on purpose to see them that I might assure you on my own observation of their good Health. Their little table was set for Breakfast and they were all neat & clean & in fine spirits. Mrs. Parks [probably a temporary house-

John Wesley Hunt
Portrait attributed to G. P. A. Healy
Courtesy of Julia Duke Henning

Catherine Hunt
Portrait copy by Alfred Domene,
at Hunt-Morgan House
(Original painting by unknown artist)

Catherine and John W. Hunt's daughter,
Henrietta Hunt Morgan, holding her
son, John Hunt Morgan

Portrait by unknown artist
Courtesy of Edward James Mathews

Hopemont

keeper] appears to me to be particularly attentive to them, and all of them very fond of her."

In 1810 John enrolled eleven-year-old Mary in Miss Hay's boarding school in New Brunswick, New Jersey, where between sessions she could visit her grandparents. Mary's mother and father accompanied her to New Jersey and after a brief visit said good-by in Philadelphia. "She bore the separation with great *magnimmity*, indeed," her grandmother observed, "as she is by no means devoid of sensibility. I give her great credit for her behaviour ever since her parting from you at Philadelphia. She felt her situation, it is very evident, but resisted her feelings so as to behave with propriety." Writing home the first time, Mary displayed the same spirit. "Having nothing to do this afternoon I thought I would write and let you know we were all well. . . . Miss Hay's school began yesterday. I was detained from going on account of the weather's being bad. It is snowing and has been all day. . . . Tell Sister I shall expect her to write frequently to me. I will exert myself very much to please both Grand Mama and Miss Hay. . . . My duty to Papa, and love to Sister and Brother. That Health & happiness may attend you through life, is the sincere wish of your ever affectionate Daughter."

Never very happy at Miss Hay's, after two years Mary persuaded her grandmother to remove her. As soon as John learned this, he mailed a letter directing Mary to return to school immediately. The thirteen-year-old girl "read her letter, gave it to her Grandmama & flew upstairs to give vent to *her grief*. However, her Grandmama soon comforted her by saying she should not on any consideration part with her untill her Papa came." Mary's eastern relatives determined to convince her father that she could study French and music just as well in Trenton and experience more of the real world than she could by staying with "twenty or thirty rude girls."

They assured her parents that Mary was "a very good girl, very industrious & attentive." John relented and Mary remained at grandmother's several months before returning to Kentucky.

When Theodosia was fourteen, it was her turn to go eastward for polishing. During the period in 1814 when the public buildings in Washington were burned and there were fears of wider raids the family was concerned for her safety in New Jersey. She stayed with her grandparents until the danger subsided, then returned to school. She was quite satisfied at grandmother's. "Theodosia is perfectly contented & happy & is a very good girl; has made herself three short gowns & several other things. Her Grandma gives her a music lesson every day & she already plays Little Bo Peep quite briskly." She liked Miss Hay's school no better than Mary, however. Uncle Wilson called there and found her dissatisfied and lonely. John allowed her to be withdrawn, and back at grandmother's house the relatives laughed heartily at her contrast of the meager table set by Miss Hay with Miss Hay's own appearance "which is the most perfect health equal to good corn fed at best seasons of the year."

When John's attention turned from family to business during this period, his thoughts were not only of thoroughbreds, but also of hemp. Hemp had been introduced into North America in the early days of the colonial period by the English, who used it to make strong sails and rope for sailing vessels. Early in Kentucky's history settlers grew hemp for the making of clothing, linen, and rope for domestic use. The Bluegrass region was well adapted to the enterprise, and Kentucky produced most of the hemp grown in the United States until the 1850s. The first hemp factory in Kentucky had been established by John Hamilton in Lexington in 1790. Hamilton's factory produced rope, and by 1800 there were five rope-making factories in operation in

Kentucky. These establishments, called ropewalks, consisted of long, narrow buildings where hemp fiber was spun into yarn, then twisted into rope. Sometimes the yarn was wound on reels and shipped to New Orleans or the Atlantic coast, where it was made into cordage.

Early in the nineteenth century, Kentucky manufacturers found a new demand for hempen materials. The invention of the cotton gin by Eli Whitney in 1793 had opened the way for a tremendous increase in cotton production. The cotton was ginned, pressed into bales, and held together by strong binding made of hemp—a 300-pound bale of cotton requiring about fifteen pounds of hemp. A woven material called cotton bagging (but made of hemp) was held around the cotton bale by hempen cordage called bale rope. Southern planters had been importing these supplies when the Kentucky manufacturers entered the business. By 1809, however, Kentucky claimed to be providing nearly all the bagging and bale rope used in the South. Close proximity to a large surplus of raw materials and the location upriver from southern plantations were stimulants to the manufacture of cotton bagging in Kentucky. In 1813 there were eight bagging factories in operation in Lexington, producing about 480,000 yards annually. A majority of the factories produced both bagging and bale rope. Such an establishment was likely to consist of storage houses, a spinning house, a weaving house, and a ropewalk.

John W. Hunt became a pioneer in the manufacture of cotton bagging. His experience is one of the best illustrations of his entrepreneurial skill. He was one of the first, if not the first, in Kentucky to enter the profitable business. On July 21, 1801, John expressed an interest in the hemp industry in a letter to his father. On December 21, 1801, he wrote his cousin Abijah inquiring about the sale of cotton bagging, cordage, and twine in Natchez. The latter replied that the manufacture of cotton bagging would become "more productive than any other business yet established in your country as there is, and ever will be, a very great Consumption of that article in this lower Country, and it will always command money." Abijah asked John to send 6,000 yards on trial and stipulated that, if it proved strong enough, he would contract for 15,000 to 20,000 yards per year.

By April 28, 1803, John's manufacture of cotton bagging had begun. Abijah, convinced that John would be able to undersell those who imported cotton bagging from Europe, advised that contracts be made with planters and cotton accepted as payment. The cotton could then be shipped to New York or Philadelphia to a house on which John could draw for the proceeds. Abijah continued: "If your bagging is such as I conceive it is—at least 40 inches wide very strong and heavy—say to weigh 2 lb. to the yd. it is worth from 35 to 37 1/2 Cents per yard by the quantity at Natchez." In addition to the quantity he had already ordered from England, Abijah offered once more to buy 6,000 yards from John.

Henry Turner, a commission merchant in Natchez, was equally encouraging about the prospects of the sale of bagging. In the summer of 1803, he stated that the previous winter he had imported 25,000 yards of heavy bagging from Europe. The purchase price, shipping charges, freight, and duties amounted to an enormous expense. Turner was certain that Hunt's location would enable him to sell his product at a lower price than imported bagging brought. In November Turner complained that John had made a sale of bagging and had not sent any to him. A few years later, when Turner had seen a sample of Hunt's bagging, he wrote that it was "superior to any I have ever seen from Europe, in point of strength. There appears indeed to be but one Fault, that is the Selvedge is a little rough & uneven, this you Can Easily Remedy."

For his foreman and partner Hunt chose John Brand, an experienced hemp manufacturer. Brand had manufactured sailcloth in Scotland before emigrating to the United States. In partnership with Hunt until 1810,

Brand managed production while Hunt took charge of marketing and purchasing. Hemp fiber was obtained from farmers around Lexington and other Bluegrass towns such as Danville and Paris.

Southern industry in general made intensive use of slave labor and to the profitable operation of hemp factories it was thought essential. Hunt worked slaves in his factory for eleven years and found the system to his economic advantage. Table 1 shows how his slave-holdings increased during the years in which he was a man-

TABLE 1

SLAVE-HOLDINGS OF JOHN W. HUNT, 1802–1814

Year	Slaves 16 yrs. old & under	All Slaves
1802	6	12
1803	17	36
1804	22	41
1805	24	41
1807	24	41
1808	18	33
1809	46	77
1810	46	77
1811	46	76
1812	40	76
1814	2	8

Source: Kentucky Tax Records, 1802–1814. Tax returns are missing for 1806, and for Hunt in 1813.

ufacturer. In 1802, before he entered the business, he owned twelve slaves for use as household servants and farm laborers. During 1803 the number of his slaves increased to thirty-six. Between 1808 and 1809 it more than doubled, possibly indicating that he expanded his operation considerably at the time. In 1814, after selling out, he owned only eight slaves.

Negro men, women, boys, and possibly girls worked in Hunt's factory. Over half the Negroes he owned were sixteen years of age or younger. He bought many young boys, several of them under twelve; there are bills of sale for over fifty boys acquired between 1803 and 1812. Most of the sales were in the Lexington area. In July 1804 he purchased two boys—Reuben, about twelve, and Harry, about ten, for $500. In April 1805 he paid John Postlethwaite $500 for two boys—Robin, nineteen, and Harvey, eleven or twelve. In 1806 he gave $256 for Willis, eleven; $270 for Elijah, about ten; $400 for Eliza, about fifteen; $650 for Bill, about nineteen, and Charles, about nine. Nearly all the bills of sale were in Hunt's handwriting with the seller's signature at the bottom. An example:

Recd. October 21st 1803 of John W. Hunt Two hundred & fifty dollars in full for a Negro boy named Isaac aged about nine years which I delivered to him the eleventh day of last August, and do obligate myself my heirs &c. to warrant and defend the Title of said boy to Hunt his heirs &c. forever.

William T. Banton

At this time prime field hands sold for about $425 in Virginia, $600 in Charleston and New Orleans.

About one-fifth of all industrial slaves were rented by employers from the masters. Hunt's use of rented slaves was near the southern average. The town directory for 1806 stated that his factory employed between forty and fifty workers. At this time he owned forty-one slaves, several of whom were employed in domestic work. Therefore it appears that Hunt hired about ten to twenty slaves for factory labor.

Apparently Hunt provided well for the slaves he owned and hired. They were cared for by the family physician, Elisha Warfield, and by the family dentist and surgeon, Andrew McCalla. Accounts with these physicians for the years during which Hunt was a manufacturer have many entries on care for the factory slaves. For example, on July 23, 1808, McCalla bled the weaver Isaac, who belonged to John Brand. The fee was 25 cents. On December 27, 1808, he bled Nelly at the factory for the same price. In January 1809 he extracted one of Tarlton's teeth for 25 cents.

In common with Kentucky hemp factories in general, Hunt's establishment used the "task system" to encourage diligence among the workers. In September 1810 he was in Philadelphia on a business trip when he received a letter from his foreman, John Brand:

Except Watt & John Scott the weavers has done tolerably well last week & them that was behind has done their three piece[s], them two has been falling behind since ever you went away, Watt is now thirty one dressings behind & John twenty six, Watt has behaved so insufferable since your absence that I have determined to put up with it no longer he goes of[f] at any time in the week & stays a day or a day & a half, & trifles his time even when at home, I told them all yesterday that them who is behind must do their three piece[s] a week untill their work is square & who ever did not I was determined to punish. . . .

Major has been off work this week or two on account of getting two of his fingers a little mashed with the callender.

During an absence in June 1813 Hunt received a similar letter from Thomas H. Burbridge, his foreman at the time:

I announce to you with pleasure, that we are doing as well I believe as could be expected, we have had manny of the boy's sick, and at this time there is three of the weavers off sick, we have . . . from 2 to 3 of the spinners constantly off since you left home there complaints has been much as usual Roy has been sick ever since you started and I doubt very much wheather he lives much longer or not he is very low with an inflamation of the lungs. The boy's has all behaved well excepting Umphry who got offended and started off one evening and was caught and brought home the next night.

Running away was not unusual among the slaves. Hunt's account with the county jail for eight months in the latter part of 1808 and early 1809 reveals that during this period ten of his slaves were confined. Five were seized by the town watchmen on February 4, 1809, and placed in jail. No offense is mentioned—they may have run away, but they were probably caught out of quarters without a pass. The account of a boy confined in November 1808 specifically mentions that he had run away. In September 1813 Hunt wrote to his brother Wilson in Philadelphia requesting him to be on the lookout for a runaway slave named Charles. If Charles were to be found in Philadelphia, Wilson had instructions to have him delivered to the house of Roger B. Taney (later Chief Justice) in Frederick, Maryland, where John was visiting at the time.

Fires were common in southern factories and often arson was suspected as a means of servile protest. The dry hemp fiber made hemp factories especially vulnerable. In 1806 Hart & Dodge's ropewalk burned in Lexington, and James Weir's factory was "chiefly consumed" shortly before January 1812. The Hunt factory burned twice, and each time the fire was blamed on arsonists. The first fire was in November 1807, with the establishment either badly damaged or destroyed. A slave boy belonging to Green Clay, a cousin of Henry Clay's father, was convicted of setting the fire and was sentenced to be hanged. The state auditor of public accounts was directed to pay Clay $350 in compensation after the death sentence was pronounced.

The rebuilt Hunt factory burned for a second time during an outbreak of fires in Lexington. On January 7, 1812, at about 5:30 A.M., the citizens of the town were called out to extinguish a fire in the smokehouse of a "Mr. Huston" (probably William Huston, saddler). There was little damage. On the next morning at the same hour fire was discovered in Hunt's factory. It was not checked until it had destroyed the spinning house and store house containing between seventy and eighty tons of hemp. The weaving house, hackling house (where hemp fiber was dressed), and other buildings were preserved. The *American Statesman* estimated the damage at up to $20,000.

Two Negro boys of about fourteen were arrested, tried, and convicted for setting fire to the Hunt factory. They were sentenced to be hanged on February 18. After the sentencing they confessed their guilt, but they were pardoned by Governor Charles Scott because of their age and "some representations relative to the testimony, which were made to the governor." The *Kentucky Gazette* disapproved of the pardon: "What is this, but declaring that infancy is a protection for crime, and that boys may burn houses with impunity?" The editorial stated that arson had become very common and "punishment should be certain by way of example."

John's brothers Pearson and Wilson expressed sympathy concerning the loss. However, both stated that they took consolation in knowing that John was able to support himself and his family in the manner in which they were accustomed and that the loss would not deprive his family of any comfort. Pearson advised him to abandon manufacturing and live the rest of his life on what he had already accumulated. He suggested that John could amuse himself by investing in the stock market. But at thirty-eight John was hardly ready for retirement. He rebuilt once more and continued in hemp manufacturing for two years longer.

Hunt operated his factory during a period when the rights of the United States as a neutral nation on the high seas were threatened. The Embargo and then the Nonintercourse acts, passed in an effort to gain recognition of United States rights without going to war, virtually excluded foreign hemp from the United States. Southern planters and northeastern cordage manufacturers turned to domestic sources for their supply of hemp products. Consequently the growing and manufacturing of hemp was greatly stimulated in Kentucky. By 1810 the state had thirty-eight ropewalks, more than any other in the nation, and was second only to Massachusetts in the total weight of cordage produced. In the same year, Kentucky possessed thirteen factories producing 453,750 yards of bagging valued at $159,445. And Lexington was the manufacturing center of Kentucky.

In 1812 Henry Clay expected the war against England to raise the price of Kentucky hemp, but such was not the case. From early 1811 to the latter part of 1814, the price of fiber was low, and the prices of finished products were not especially high. While imports were almost nonexistent, there was a large supply of hemp on hand at the outbreak of the war. Dealers and manufacturers of hemp were continually apprehensive that prices would fall still more once peace returned and imports resumed. The blockade decreased the demand for cordage for sailing vessels. A drop in cotton exports lessened the need for cotton bagging and bale rope. Nevertheless, large quantities of hemp were used and manufacturing in Kentucky increased. It was estimated in 1814 that during the preceding four years the number of ropewalks in the state had doubled.

Shipments by Hunt reflect the increase in the manufacture of hemp in Kentucky. During the years that Hunt's factory was in operation (1803 through 1813), he shipped hemp products to Nashville, Saint Louis, Natchez, New Orleans, Charleston, Savannah, Augusta, Philadelphia, and Baltimore. Before 1810, all shipments (except for a small quantity to Saint Louis) were to points south. By 1810, the Embargo and Nonintercourse acts had made upriver shipments profitable. Hunt was one of the earliest in this upriver trade. In 1810 he began wagoning hemp fiber and yarns to Maysville for shipment by keelboat to Pittsburgh. From there the cargoes went to Benjamin B. Howell & Company, a commission firm in Philadelphia. The fiber and yarns were used for the manufacture of cordage in Philadelphia. Before the year ended Howell had sold $16,396.30 worth of hemp and yarns for Hunt and still had yarn on hand.

Hunt continued the manufacture of hemp for three more years but in 1810 he redirected the capital and energy he had invested in the horse industry into a new career—that of commission merchant. He used his established connections and reputation, as well as a thorough knowledge of the market system, to ship hemp and other products belonging to neighboring merchants and manufacturers to Philadelphia and New Orleans. The commission merchant usually served several clients and also bought and sold on his own account. He made transportation arrangements and paid storage, wharfage, and carting fees. He sold goods or forwarded them to the seller. Liability was with the owner. The commission agent usually received a 5 percent commission on all goods handled.

One of the most important functions of the commission merchant was to provide credit. Hunt stimulated the economy of central Kentucky by making Philadelphia credit available. In December 1810 he opened an exchange account with Benjamin B. Howell. By an agreement that may have lasted until March 1816, Howell was to make advances to Hunt for use in the purchase of yarn and saltpeter in Kentucky. Then when the goods were sold in Philadelphia, the amount of sale was credited to Hunt's balance in the exchange account. Howell benefited by the increase in shipments. Hunt used part of the money advanced by Howell to purchase Kentucky produce for shipment on his own account. The remainder he advanced, in turn, to certain manufacturers who agreed to pay him a 5 percent commission for shipping their products. During the four-year period between 1811 and 1815, Hunt's arrangement with

Howell stimulated and helped expedite the exportation of Kentucky hemp fiber and products, saltpeter, and tobacco.

Accounts rendered for the exchange account between them indicate something of the volume of business. On December 23, 1812, Hunt had over $1,000 to his favor in the sales account but had $17,272.59 to his debit in the exchange account. This reveals that as of that day, Howell had advanced him $17,272.59 for investment. An account rendered on October 9, 1814, for an undesignated period before that time shows that Hunt had drawn on Howell for $117,357 and had paid him $98,492. Therefore, on that day Howell was advancing him over $17,000. Making this Philadelphia credit available to central Kentucky was a considerable contribution to the state's economy.

In 1811 Hunt participated in the saltpeter trade both as a commission merchant and on his own. War clouds were gathering and saltpeter, used in the making of gunpowder, was sold at a considerable profit in Philadelphia. Writing drafts on the exchange account with Howell, Hunt purchased saltpeter and made advances as a commission agent. In the spring of 1811 he purchased large quantities on his own account in Kentucky for 20 cents per pound and sold them in Philadelphia for 36 to 38 cents. In June 1811 he had sold 117 barrels for $11,554.35. This investment was one of Hunt's most profitable in the period before he entered the stock market. During the War of 1812, Hunt invested no further in saltpeter. The war created a great demand, causing prices to rise in the West to the point that saltpeter cost nearly as much in Kentucky as it did in Pennsylvania. Rising prices in the West made shipment to the East far less profitable.

While Hunt and Howell made some minor investments in tobacco and cotton during the War of 1812, Hunt concentrated most of his energy at this time on the business of dealing in hempen yarn as a commission merchant. Even though prices remained at a low level, there was, as we have seen, a large volume of business. Hunt attempted to make contracts with the navy for yarn. Apparently his only success was when Henry Clay, as agent for Hart & Company of Lexington, included a quantity of Hunt's yarn in a navy contract in 1813.

Although he continued dealing in hemp, John stopped manufacturing late in 1813. In November of that year, he advertised in the *Kentucky Gazette* to sell his factory slaves:

FOR SALE,

Sixty Negroes,

THE Subscriber having determined to abandon the manufacture of *Bagging*, will offer at *public sale* at the Hotel in Lexington, on Wednesday the 22d day of December next, all the Negroes employed in said manufactory consisting of

Men, Boys & women.

These negroes were selected with the view of being retained in my own service; purchasers will now have the opportunity of being benefitted by my experience.

At about the same time, he disposed of the factory to Luke Usher & Company, who continued bagging manufacture in the facility. When he relinquished that part of the business, Hunt again demonstrated his remarkable ability to redirect his investments at the right moment. It was an opportune time; a few years later there would have been no buyer for the factory. Peace brought a renewal of foreign competition, and consequently the price of bagging and other hempen goods declined. Bagging factories closed in Lexington until in 1820 only one was still in operation.

Many entrepreneurs invested in a wide variety of ventures at the same time. Hunt was involved in many lesser projects during the period 1803 to 1816. He shipped flour and other Kentucky food products to New Orleans; sold whiskey and other produce in Saint Louis; transported over 31,000 pounds of ginseng by steamboat from Louisville via New Orleans to John Jacob Astor in New York; speculated in the wholesaling of general merchandise; and held temporary interest in an ironworks and a saltworks.

The increasing value of Hunt's bank deposits and withdrawals are one indication of the increasing volume of his business during these years. Between August 1812 and February 1813, he deposited $13,241.62 with the Kentucky Insurance Company and as of February 3, 1813, had withdrawn in checks or cash all but $854.65. Between June and August of 1813, over $13,000 was deposited in the Bank of Pennsylvania and as of August 12, 1813, Hunt had a balance in his favor of $11,135.21. Between November 1813 and January 1814 he deposited and withdrew over $100,000 from his account with the Lexington branch of the Bank of Kentucky. In a roughly comparable period in late 1815 and early 1816, he deposited over $850,000 in the same bank and as of February 21, 1816 had a balance of $11,719.99.

The economy of Lexington had become increasingly diversified since the turn of the century. By 1816 many merchants besides Hunt were investing capital reserves in manufacturing. James Weir, for example, invested mercantile capital in a bagging factory, ropewalk, and cotton mill. The booming hemp industry was only one part of a general movement toward industrialization. In 1810 Lexington had a number of factories—eight processing cotton, three wool, and one producing oilcloth. By 1816 there was a steam engine manufactory and six steam mills were in operation.

John W. Hunt had a major impact on the industrialization of Lexington. He was among the first to manufacture cotton bagging. He marketed in Nashville, Saint Louis, Natchez, New Orleans, Charleston, Savannah, Augusta, Philadelphia, and Baltimore. Other Lexington manufacturers used his connections. When John Brand opened his own factory in 1811, he employed Hunt's agents in Natchez, New Orleans, and Augusta. Hunt helped open the upriver trade in 1810 by shipping hemp and yarn up the Ohio. Through this innovation he indirectly advanced the cordage industry in Philadelphia.

As a commission merchant after 1810, Hunt stimulated the western economy by transporting hemp fiber and products, saltpeter, and tobacco to outside markets. He secured large amounts of Philadelphia credit to stimulate manufacturing and commercial agriculture in Kentucky. By 1816 Hunt had acquired considerable capital and had become Kentucky's leading entrepreneur. As an innovator, he had made a significant contribution to the economic development of the Ohio and Mississippi valleys and the nation.

6

HOPEMONT

IN THE NINETEENTH CENTURY urban merchants and financiers often set the tone of society. Social leadership and paternalism had been recognized for centuries as part of the merchant's role. Entrepreneurs such as John W. Hunt spread civilization and stimulated culture. They supported institutions of higher learning, patronized the arts, sustained philanthropies, and served the church. Often they set the example in taste, consumption, and manners.

Hunt contributed to the architectural splendor of early Lexington with the beautiful family home he constructed. In February 1814, at the age of forty, he purchased a lot at the northwest corner of Mill and Second streets from Thomas January for $3,000. Hopemont, which stands today as a handsome example of Georgian architecture, was built on this site. Tradition holds that Hopemont was designed by Benjamin Henry Latrobe. The house now serves as a museum, maintained by the Blue Grass Trust for Historic Preservation.

Hopemont was a large house, and for good reason— the babies kept coming, at least one every two years. After Abraham in 1809, there were Catherine, Thomas, Francis Key, Anne, and finally in 1819, the twelfth, Robert. The large family inspired comment. Cousin Wilson P. Hunt wrote from Louisville: "Please to give my love to Mrs. Hunt and to *all the children*. I must speak of them yet in this way. I did not see Eleanor and Henrietta in coming away, and where there are so many that is not so much to wonder at." Brother Wilson observed: "You have indeed a large family, and I am very glad that you possess ample means to provide for all your children in such manner that they will have it in their power to live comfortably." John's friend Horace Holley, president of Transylvania University, congratulated him for having "a peculiarly amiable and excellent family, a family uncommonly happy."

Hopemont was furnished with the finest furniture, and portraits by noted artists adorned the walls. Knowing their reputation for good taste, Thomas January asked John and Catherine to procure wallpaper for him: "The fashion of the paper I cannot pretend to prescribe but rely confidently upon you, but more particularly on *Mrs.* Hunt's taste for its Beauty." From Philadelphia came Venetian blinds, a mantel glass, and other items. From London was brought "an elegantly ornamented Square Pianoforte with Circular Corners and Drawers."

With twelve children, several servants, and frequent guests, Hopemont was alive with activity. Just home from a trip, Mrs. Hunt complained: "I am in the same bustle, Abram and his wife are here and Mary. Company is comeing all day and part of the night. Catherine's return too, makes a great stir. Receiving visits and returning them takes much time." Another responsibility was managing the house servants. "I wish we could do without them," Mrs. Hunt exclaimed recklessly. "Hang them all, I say." The children played the piano and other instruments, rode horseback, and romped on the Transylvania University lawn. One of Henrietta's playmates was Henrietta Holley, daughter of the university president.

Mrs. Hunt retained her beauty in maturity. At fifty, the mother of twelve could still turn the heads of the men in Philadelphia. Caroline Warfield, a friend of her daughter Anne, related: "Oh, I must tell you what a belle Mrs. H. is; she looks so well and spruce that the *Bachelors* are particularly *attentive;* one sent her a spring bottom chair, another got a *new ring,* and another was so kind as to give her his room whilst he is absent!! She throws Anne & I in the back grounds. One evening Mr. Warmsby (aged seventy) *did* waltz with Anne. They will all be in dumps today at dinner when they find she has gone and I am afraid I will be too lonely. However I will force them in good spirits by talking of her."

Catherine was close enough to John to confide in him freely, but she did not relate to him as an equal. She deferred to his wishes and approached him with respect. In her charming letters she never used his first name. Away on a journey, she wrote: "I received three letters from you, Dear Husband, for which you have my sincere thanks." In 1828 John strongly encouraged her to bathe in an eastern mineral springs for her health. After nearly three days at the springs she could not bring herself to go into the water. "I fear you will be hurt, My dear Mr. Hunt at my leaving the Branch so soon," she apologized. "However, if I return in good health you will be satisfied." Catherine accepted a subordinate role but she did not fear her husband. She often wrote in a teasing tone. After an exciting day in Saint Louis in 1831, she wrote: "I suppose *you* are enjoying sweet Solitude and peace and feasting on Strawberries."

Catherine was a conscientious, loving mother. During a visit to Saint Louis, she was concerned about the youngest son back at Hopemont. "I hope Robert is a good boy and that he comes home as soon as school is out and employ himself at home. He must go clean and neat. Take care of his Leghorn Hat. Only wear it when he goes to Church or down Street and always keep it upstairs or in the office. Put it away himself." A week later she told Robert: "I hope you will be a good boy and much at home and when at home well employed. . . ." On the way home, she commented: "Love to Robert. poor fellow he complains of being lonesome."

John continued in good health; his correspondence contains few references to illness on his part. On the other hand, Catherine had delicate health during the latter half of her life. Relatives in Trenton frequently expressed concern over her physical condition. John believed travel was good therapy so he encouraged it. On a journey to Saint Louis in 1831, Mrs. Hunt found herself on a steamboat for the first time. On the trip up the Mississippi River she was quite nervous and could hardly sleep. "When I look around me and think that only a plank separates me from Eternity, Oh how I shudder," she worried. "I shall rejoice when I am released from Steamboats." By the time she started home, however, Catherine had gained courage and slept soundly. At first she considered Saint Louis too scattered for a town and *"not handsome."* But the old French houses with porches all around were a curiosity and the French ladies were affable and cheerful, "all Life and Spirits." Mrs. Hunt enjoyed the church services in Saint Louis but deplored the fact that many gentlemen in the town were making merry and seemed content even though they had not seen their wives for several years.

In August 1828 Mrs. Hunt and Anne were in Philadelphia. Mrs. Hunt hoped to return home via canal to Pittsburgh and evidently thence by steamboat. Concerning stage travel she commented: "I am determined not to encounter the Maill Stage, I had enough of that through Virginia." She was impressed with the church services in Philadelphia. Everyone united in the service, and "the Churches were filled to overflowing young and old; all seem hearty in the Cause."

On one eastern trip, Mrs. Hunt rode on the country's first railway, the Baltimore and Ohio. She reported: "I had a Ride on the rail Road and was delighted. It is finished from Ellicott's Mills to Baltimore. Nine or ten

Cars are going. It is a gay sight to see them all filled, inside and outside, the Top and every part with gay Ladys and Gentlemen."

The children were aware that their father expected a great deal of them. Francis Key, facing commencement exercises at Kenyon College, hoped "to *sustain* the honor of the family, if I cannot *advance* it." The sons realized that John demanded singleminded attention to business on the part of his agents. When one went on an errand for him, no time was to be lost in reporting back. Exceptional lenience was shown in January 1823, when Charlton, the eldest son, was in western Kentucky on a legal mission. "I this moment recd. your letter under date of the 28 Dec," said John. "I was pleased to learn you reached Hopkinsville in safety. Upon your return it will not be necessary to be in a hurry. Therefore do not wish you to travel in bad weather, and if you desire to return by Frankfort have not the smallest objection."

The father was somewhat careful about spending his money. In 1834 a Lexington dentist billed him for $11.50 and $51.50 for dental care for two of the children. He considered the sums exorbitant. By arbitration the bills were lowered to $8.00 and $32.00. In 1839 a close friend in Cincinnati jokingly returned a letter on which John had charged himself double postage: "For once in my long acquaintance I have it in my power to say to you, you have taken yourself in." This parsimonious quality was generally instilled in the children, except for John Wilson, the second son.

From an early age John Wilson was a rowdy boy. At seven big sister Mary commented: "John W. goes to school & has grown so *wild* & *noisy* that you would be astonished if this letter should omit" mention of him. At thirteen, to one of his brothers, he was "a bad, a very bad boy." At fourteen he was sent to the church school of Episcopal Bishop Philander Chase in Worthington, Ohio, where it was hoped the stern discipline of the bishop would reform him. For the first few weeks at

76

school John W. seemed "highly exemplary" in conduct. However, when the bishop announced that he would be favored with a coveted trip into Chillicothe, his peers ran to the bishop's son, who was assistant headmaster, with the report that John W. had been sinning in secret. They accused him of buying liquor at taverns in the town on the way from classes, which were held across town from the boarding house. "Where is John at this moment?" asked Philander Chase, Jr. "He has not returned from classes," was the reply.

"I immediately rode back towards the town," the assistant headmaster recorded, "and met John returning, as it appears, even then from the tavern. I led him home to my Father. The scene that followed it is unnecessary to state. It was such as, whether he informs or not, he never will forget. . . . He left us the next morning clandestinely. . . . He said once to one of his mates I have been told, that were he ever to run away he should go to an uncle's near Philadelphia." If John W. ran to Uncle Wilson, no doubt he received the same kind of advice as he had heard from his father.

Somehow, John W., who was extremely handsome, managed to settle down enough to study medicine. In November 1826, when he was nineteen, he wrote home from Philadelphia thanking his father for paying his debts and announcing that he had borrowed another $175. "I have no doubt but that you will have the kindness to pay the amount but will as certainly think me a sadly extravagant fellow. I can only repeat my asseverations that I endeavor to be economical & am not sensible in what particular my expences exceed those of my companions or of many particulars in which I am improperly distributive." Two years later he was still apologetic: "It appears as though my demands on you would never cease. I can offer as the only extenuation a review of my course for 2 years past, which have been spent in the most devoted attention to my profession."

John was a generous father; his wedding gift to each

daughter was a carriage with horses. However, there were limits. In 1832 John W. drew on his father for $260 without permission, and his father rebuked him: "I had hoped after the candid manner you had been treated by me as regards your expenses it would have restrained you" but "you intend pursueing your own course at all hazards disregarding my advise." What good will money be to you "if it should be at the expence of your reputation, the sacrifice of the interest of the family or my comfort? What you do with so much money astonishes me, at any rate if this course is persisted in by you all intercourse between us must cease."

A few months later, at the age of twenty-five, John W. began practicing medicine in New Orleans and was reconciled with his father. He had been in New Orleans about a year when he and a lawyer friend, Charles M. Conrad (later to become a United States Congressman and Senator) became rivals for the affection of a Miss Carleton. In the presence of the young lady, Conrad insulted Hunt's good name by insinuating that Hunt drank to excess and used language unbecoming a gentleman. Confronted, Conrad further charged John W. with having "loose sentiments" and Parisian manners. In the face of such insults John W. was forced by the custom of the day to take to the field to protect his honor. On July 25, 1833, the two gentlemen met and Hunt fell. "The bullet entered his head immediately above the right temple and near the forehead," and he died instantly. In the Lexington Cemetery the family, already saddened that year by the premature death of daughter Catherine, placed a monument with the following words: "Cut off in the Prime of Life and in the Fulness of Health/His Untimely Fate Drew Tears from Strangers Eyes/Mysterious are the Ways of God."

The Hunt children were provided the best education available. In addition to Mary and Theodosia's New Jersey schooling, at least two of the girls attended Mary Beck's Academy for Young Ladies in Lexington. Mrs.

Beck taught "every branch of what is considered as an English classical education, combining the useful, the ornamental, and the solid." All six boys attended Transylvania University and at least three received degrees there (Charlton, Abraham D., and Francis Key). Charlton studied law under Roger B. Taney before Taney became Chief Justice of the United States. Francis Key graduated from Kenyon College in Gambier, Ohio. Robert, like his deceased uncle and namesake, attended Princeton. John W., and later Robert, studied medicine in Paris.

The coming of the steamboat era in 1815 put inland Lexington under an economic disadvantage. The town was unable to compete with Pittsburgh, Cincinnati, and Louisville once these cities began to expand production in response to the availability of cheap, easy transportation of goods. The growth rate of Lexington's trade and manufacturing slowly declined and the rapid population growth halted. From 1810 to 1820 the population increased only from 4,326 to 5,279. By 1830 Lexington had lost its supremacy as the commercial and manufacturing center of the West.

Hunt may have sensed the coming decline in August 1815, when he wrote: "The changes in the circumstances of a number of our inhabitants since you left this [place] is very great, and the Town is not improving as rapidly as it was, altho several good houses have been put up this season." In 1816 Hunt made an important shift in investment, which had the effect of shielding him against the decline of the local economy. To the end of his life, he supported efforts to help Lexington regain her strength, while personally, his fortune continued to soar through investments in banking, government stock, and insurance.

Hunt's transfer to banking paralleled the national tendency of aggressive, prosperous merchants to lead in the development of finance. Many merchants went into banking after 1815 because trade profits failed to reach previous levels. John's shift also reflected the national trend toward specialization in business. During the period before the Civil War, the varied tasks of the pioneer merchant were gradually divided among specialists. Common carriers, wholesale merchants, retailers, brokers, and others came to perform separate functions. Like Philadelphia merchant Stephen Girard, Hunt came increasingly to specialize in banking and finance after the War of 1812.

Hunt supported expansive banking as a means of providing adequate credit and currency for western business. His activities advanced the growth of the regional and national economy. In a limited way he had been involved in banking from its earliest days in Kentucky. In 1806 he was elected one of four directors of the Kentucky Insurance Company, the first banking institution in the state. Chartered by the legislature in 1802, ostensibly to insure boats and cargoes on inland waters, the concern had also acquired monopolistic banking privileges. This aspect of its activities occasioned considerable opposition culminating in a charter revision in 1804, which permitted organization of the Bank of Kentucky in 1806. Nevertheless, the company survived as a strong institution, and its notes circulated above par. The charter ran out in 1818, when its nonbanking privileges were extended for two years. Hunt did considerable business (deposits and withdrawals) with the firm from 1808 to 1813.

In 1806 the legislature chartered the Bank of Kentucky, the first institution in the state designed solely for banking purposes. The Bank of Kentucky's notes soon made up a significant part of the circulating medium of the state. Beginning in 1816, Hunt speculated in Bank of Kentucky and other western bank notes, which were circulating in the East at a discount. His agents in Philadelphia and Baltimore bought the paper at a discount in these cities and mailed it to Hunt, who then presented the notes to the bank of issue.

Between March 20 and April 4, 1816, McEuen, Hale & Davidson of Philadelphia purchased $14,712.20 in notes on the Bank of Kentucky and sent them to Hunt. On May 10 Simon Gratz & Brothers forwarded to him $482 in Kentucky bank notes bought at 6 percent discount and $165 in Ohio bank notes at 9 percent discount. Between June 19 and August 13 McEuen, Hale & Davidson transmitted $14,889.16 worth of Kentucky notes and Hunt's brokers made smaller purchases of the notes of banks in Ohio, Tennessee, Virginia, North and South Carolina, and New Orleans.

In 1816 Hunt also speculated in the stock of the Second Bank of the United States. A few days after Congress chartered the Second Bank of the United States in April, the Gratz brothers warned that Hunt and his friends should exert all their influence to obtain a branch at Lexington since Louisville interests had sent a petition to Philadelphia and were doing everything they could to supplant Lexington as the site for a branch in Kentucky. Lexington acquired its branch, but by July 1817 Louisville also had one. James Morrison was president of the Lexington branch and two of the directors were John W. Hunt and his future son-in-law, John H. Hanna.

On July 4, 1816, the subscription books for stock in the Bank of the United States were opened in Lexington and nineteen other American communities. The three commissioners appointed by President James Madison to superintend the subscriptions in Lexington were John W. Hunt, John Tilford, and Thomas Prather. Greeting subscribers at the office of the Kentucky Insurance Company, the commissioners sold 9,587 shares to 710 people. Lexington was the eighth city in the nation and first in the West in the number of subscriptions.

As early as June 6, 1816, Hunt had decided that national bank stock was a profitable speculation. Simon Gratz & Brothers advised that it would be a good investment and would pay off within three years. On July 2 John's brother Wilson wrote: "I do not expect the Shares of the Bank United States will be sold by the Subscribers for a profit within Eighteen Months, after that period, I am equally confident that the Shares will yield, a handsome profit to the Subscribers, as my acquaintances have the same opinion of the Stock, very few of them will be Subscribers to the Bank." In June John was buying up government stock (that is, funded debt of the United States) to be used in making payments for national bank subscriptions. On June 6 the Gratz brothers purchased $12,500 worth of 6 percent stock at 99¾ percent. On July 2 brother Wilson learned that a certificate for $200,000 worth of 6 percent stock had been transmitted to John for the purpose of subscription to the Bank of the United States. On the same day, McDonald & Ridgely of Baltimore, having received $50,000 in bills of exchange on Philadelphia, payable in four months, invested it for John in 6 percent stock at 103½ percent. Perhaps John sold part of this government stock to Kentuckians for use in making payments to the national bank; it is possible that most of it was disposed of in that manner. Regardless of whether he sold the stock or invested it in the Bank of the United States himself, he profited by the speculation.

Unfortunately the records do not reveal how many shares were initially purchased by individuals during the subscription in July 1816. Hunt made a loan of $100,000 to James Prentiss, a well-known Lexington speculator, who had begun to invest heavily in the Kentucky Insurance Company. Prentiss, acting as the agent for the company as well as in his own behalf, purchased 3,306 shares of Bank of the United States stock which had been subscribed in the names of sundry persons. John's brother Pearson Hunt, in Trenton, assisted Prentiss so that he could repay the loan without selling the stock. When the price of national bank stock rose, Pearson commented that Prentiss made a small fortune. Prentiss requested that John not "hint to any one the nature—magnitude of our transaction."

It is unclear how John profited from the deal. The agreement makes it plain that John was not a partner in the speculation. If the stock sold for more than the loan, Prentiss was to receive all over the amount of the loan. It seems most likely that John was speculating in the exchange rate. Kentucky Insurance Company notes were selling at 7 percent discount in Philadelphia. If he lent Prentiss depreciated western paper and received good eastern bank notes in return, he could have made about 7 percent profit. In addition, there very well could have been arrangements between John Hunt and James Prentiss which are not revealed by the documents. It does appear that John made considerable money dealing with Prentiss. John's brother Wilson wrote: "Some of the Gentlemen in your Town say you have made a moderate fortune by your transactions [with Prentiss]." By the spring of 1817, Prentiss had become the majority stockholder in the Kentucky Insurance Company and had been elected its president. Practicing fraud and deceit, he directed the company into financial ruin. In February, 1818, he left the state and the firm defaulted on its debts. However Prentiss did not act illegally before the summer of 1817, after the deal with Hunt had been closed.

In the summer of 1817 John made several purchases of Bank of the United States stock. On May 25 Wilson Hunt reported that 1,020 shares had been purchased in John's name, at a price between $125 and $130 per share. He was by far the largest individual investor in Kentucky. In Lexington that June and July Hunt purchased 267 shares on his own account from several individuals. In partnership with John D. Clifford he bought 131 shares, and with John Tilford 40 shares. The earliest printed list of subscribers, dated July 1817, shows that at the time Hunt was one of only thirty-three individuals who held at least 1,000 shares in his own name.

The price of the Bank of the United States stock rose more rapidly than Wilson Hunt and his friends had anticipated, advancing by October to a price about $20 per share above what Hunt had paid in the summer. Promptly he instructed his agents to sell. On the second and third of October, 200 shares sold for $149.50; on the fourth, 100 shares brought $150 per share; on the seventh, 985 shares went at $153. In less than five months Hunt had obtained better than 15 percent on his investment. This amounted to over $24,000.

Continuing his interest in banking, Hunt was elected president of one of the forty-six independent banks chartered by the Kentucky legislature in 1818. This was the Farmers and Mechanics Bank of Lexington, with authorized capital up to $1 million. On June 1, 1818, the stockholders met at Keen's Tavern and elected Hunt president. Cashier Matthew T. Scott opened the bank in the building formerly occupied by the Kentucky Insurance Company. Although the loss of this bank's records makes it difficult to reconstruct Hunt's role in its management, on January 1, 1819, the officers reported to the stockholders in what a newspaper called "a very flattering and satisfactory statement of the situation of the institution." The report stated:

The specie in the vaults was more than double the amount of notes in circulation, and exceeded all demands that could be made on the institution, whether on account of its notes or deposits, at least *forty-eight per cent.* The public are thus assured, that this is literally a *specie* bank, possessing the means and ability of continuing the payment of specie. After paying all expenses, and reserving a surplus fund of $6,237, the board declared a dividend at the rate of *ten per cent per annum.*

Hunt was reelected president in 1819 and 1820. When the panic of 1819 forced most of the independent banks to close because they could not pay their debts, the

Farmers and Mechanics Bank remained solvent; and after the charters of all the independent banks were repealed on February 10, 1820, it continued to pay dividends to the stockholders.

When the opportunity was presented, John continued his involvement in state bank administration. The 1806 charter of the Bank of Kentucky was repealed in 1822—two years after the Bank of the Commonwealth was authorized. The latter institution lost its financial standing in the mid-1820s. In 1834 a new Bank of Kentucky came into existence. Hunt was one of the commissioners to sell capital stock in Lexington, and in 1842 and 1843 he was a director of the bank. In 1835 he was chairman of the committee of commissioners who opened books for subscription to the stock of the newly chartered Northern Bank of Kentucky.

Hunt continued investing in banks and in government stock throughout his life. In 1818 he invested $20,000 in stock of banks in Mississippi. From 1836 through 1838, he made large purchases of stock in the Bank of Kentucky and other banks. In December 1838, Charles Macalester, his broker in Philadelphia, purchased for Hunt $13,000 worth of Bank of Kentucky stock. At his death in 1849, Hunt owned stocks and bonds appraised at $242,707. United States 6 percent bonds made up $113,245 of this, and Hunt's stock in the Northern Bank of Kentucky was valued at $55,332.

Although Hunt was spending most of his energies on the banking business, he had time for other interests as well. In 1830 John was among a group of Lexington businessmen who planned to improve transportation of goods to and from Lexington. It was hoped that a railroad connecting Lexington with the Ohio River would restore the city to a competitive position with Cincinnati, Louisville, and other cities on the river which had reaped the advantage of steamboat traffic. In January 1830 the Kentucky legislature granted a charter for such a railway, and on March 6 the Lexington and

Ohio Railroad Company was organized with Hunt as one of the directors. Building began in the fall, but engineering complications, financial difficulties, and an outbreak of cholera hindered the work so that the tracks did not reach Frankfort until January 1834. There, on the Kentucky River, the company halted construction. Not until 1851, two years after Hunt's death, was the line extended to Louisville.

In a more successful venture Hunt entered the insurance business. He was president of the Lexington Fire, Life & Marine Insurance Company for several years. The firm was chartered in March 1836, with a capitalization of $300,000. Besides fire and marine insurance it offered life insurance; it also was in the business of insuring slaves employed in factories or on farms. Hunt was one of its six directors until he replaced Thomas Smith as president at some time before August 1837, and he was still president in 1848.

During the period of prosperity and westward expansion after the War of 1812, Hunt was one of the speculators attracted to the sale of public lands in Alabama. In November 1817 he entered partnership with John McKinley, a Lexington lawyer who later became a congressman and senator from Alabama and an associate justice of the United States Supreme Court. Hunt and McKinley planned to speculate in lands in Alabama and other territories. Hunt advanced $50,000 and McKinley $4,400. McKinley was to manage purchases and sales. After each was paid interest on his advance, they were to share equally in the profits.

McKinley arrived in Alabama in time for the opening of sales at the land office in Huntsville in February 1818. Speculators had already been making purchases in the territory, but in Huntsville speculation occurred on a notorious level. Buying companies or combinations were formed to eliminate competition, but rival companies and wealthy independent investors bid against each other, driving the prices up to between $50 and

$100 per acre. One tract sold for the fantastic price of $107 per acre.

In February 1818 McKinley purchased nearly 15,000 acres of land in Alabama Territory and took up permanent residence in that area where he practiced law and entered politics. In May 1821 when the partnership was renewed, Hunt and McKinley possessed property estimated to be worth $105,443.64. This included town lots in Huntsville and Florence and a 480-acre plantation near Huntsville. In April 1825 McKinley estimated that they held property in Alabama valued at $174,338.67.

Nevertheless, neither partner seems to have been very well satisfied with the result of the venture and in 1831 they agreed to terminate it. Hunt reminded McKinley that he had agreed to extend their relationship in 1821 and 1825 at McKinley's request. "I am confident it would have been much better for me to have had my money at six per cent interest, receiving that half yearly and reloaning it," Hunt claimed. He maintained that only friendship and confidence in McKinley had persuaded him to enter the relationship in the beginning. In April 1831 Hunt traveled to Alabama to settle up with McKinley. Later Hunt told his friend William A. Leavy that the Alabama speculation could have ruined him if others had known that he was involved so deeply.

In Kentucky Hunt speculated in agricultural land and town lots. In 1823 he held title to about 5,000 acres of Kentucky land. This was the greatest extent of his holdings between 1805 to his death, and rural lands of the state were never an important source of investment for him. But town lots were. In 1823 he was taxed for eight lots in Frankfort assessed at $3,000 and for six lots in Lexington valued at $31,800. In 1835 and 1836 he acquired houses and lots in Louisville for which he paid more than $84,000. The commission firm of Hobbs & Henning rented his Louisville property, which came to include warehouses as well as dwellings and stores. In 1842 Hunt's five lots in Lexington were assessed at $25,000 and his fourteen lots in Louisville at $50,000. In addition he owned at least one town lot in Saint Louis in the early 1840s. In the 1820s and 1830s Hunt entered into several temporary mercantile and hemp manufacturing ventures. These enterprises were minor in comparison to his interest in banking, government stock, and land.

There is a well-established tradition that John W. Hunt became the first millionaire west of the Allegheny Mountains. After his death in 1849, the estate was valued at $886,989.28 (see Table 2), and with allowances for the practice of appraising below the real value of property, it appears that the legend has foundation. When Hunt reached this level of wealth is not clear. He was very well-off by 1816 when he began investing heavily in money and banking. In 1825 William Morton

TABLE 2

SUMMARY OF THE INVENTORY OF THE ESTATE OF JOHN W. HUNT, SEPTEMBER 14, 1849

Book accounts (mostly advances to Hunt's children)		$353,834.71
Stocks		242,707.00
Notes (good)		93,085.94
Notes (bad)		10,308.04
Farm land, animals, etc.		85,978.00
Bills of exchange		56,136.21
Town lots		28,479.38
Farm slaves		10,100.00
House servants		4,930.00
Miscellaneous		1,430.00
	TOTAL	$886,989.28

and Samuel Trotter owned more taxable property in Lexington than Hunt; but this does not necessarily mean that they were wealthier, for Hunt's holdings were widespread and stocks were not taxed. It appears indeed that Hunt was Kentucky's leading entrepreneur and first millionaire.

As a pioneer merchant and manufacturer Hunt had experienced the need for adequate credit and currency in the West. As a financier he worked to help provide it. However, he realized that responsibility must accompany fiscal expansion. He invested heavily in the Second Bank of the United States and approved of its efforts to restrain the state banks. In 1836, after President Andrew Jackson had destroyed the national bank, John observed: "The Jackson and Van Buren people will not rest until they put down all the solvent institutions in the Country or be put down themselves. It is wonderfull how any decent respectable man can attempt to sustain them." Hunt practiced his philosophy; when nearly all the other independent banks in Kentucky suspended specie payment and closed their doors in 1819, the bank which had Hunt as president remained solvent. Hunt's efforts to provide an adequate, sound financial system advanced the growth of the regional and national economy.

PATRIARCH

INCREASINGLY INVOLVED in community affairs, John
Hunt came to be one of central Kentucky's most prominent citizens. In 1814 James Morrison recommended
him as "a Gentleman of great wealth, enterprise and re-
spectability." Perhaps John's greatest community service was his part in the founding of the Eastern Kentucky Lunatic Asylum. Prior to the early nineteenth
century, the insane in the United States were usually
cared for in private dwellings or in jails and almshouses.
In Kentucky the poor who became mentally ill were
boarded in private homes at public expense, by order of
justices of the peace or magistrates. After 1800 humani-
tarians in Europe and America, believing that the insane were human beings, not animals, and that improving their condition might effect their cure, moved to
provide something better than the traditionally poor
custodial care. Several hospitals and care centers for the
insane were founded in the United States. In 1822 Kentucky became the second state to establish an asylum
providing care exclusively for the mentally ill.

Governor John Adair, criticizing the old system in
1821, declared that it was expensive and did not provide
an opportunity for curative treatment. He proposed the
establishment of a state asylum such as the one organized in Virginia in 1773. Adair pointed out that the in-

stitution would be valuable in providing practical experience for Transylvania University medical students. Following the governor's recommendation, the General Assembly passed "An Act to establish a Lunatic Asylum" on December 7, 1822. The preamble of the law stated that the previous legislation had not been "calculated to aid in the best manner, the restoration and final cure" of the insane.

The same act appointed Hunt as one of four commissioners to apply an appropriation of $10,000 to the purchase of ten to twenty acres of land near Lexington and the erection of stone or brick buildings to accommodate 200 patients. The commissioners bought a tract of seventeen acres and a partially constructed brick building belonging to the Fayette Hospital. This institution, founded in 1816 by fifty-five contributors, including Hunt, had been planned to offer general hospital care, but financial difficulties following the panic of 1819 had prevented its completion.

In 1824 the asylum began to serve the public. The legislature appointed a board of commissioners of ten members, including Hunt, to administer the institution. The commissioners, who elected Hunt chairman of the board and Andrew Staunton superintendent of the hospital, were authorized to examine every patient brought to the asylum. Those who were "sick or imbecile only" were refused admittance, as were those with sufficient estate to provide for their own care; and, as under the earlier system, those proved harmless before a circuit court could be kept at home at public expense. In May the public was notified that patients were being received.

Hunt continued as chairman of the board of commissioners until 1844—a period of twenty years. He received many letters from concerned relatives inquiring about the condition of patients. For instance, in 1838 a woman from Elizabethtown asked if it would help her husband if she visited him in the hospital. She also requested that Hunt inform her husband that his crops were thriving. Hunt kept the accounts of the institution and purchased its supplies, apparently keeping a close watch on operations and expenditures. From day to day his involvement took a great deal of time. An example of the kind of detail he was concerned with is his purchase, in December 1825, of a shroud and coffin for a little boy who had died at the institution.

A conscious goal of the asylum from the beginning was the cure and restoration of patients. Faculty members and students at Transylvania served as consultants, and by 1838 there was an attending physician. Letters to Hunt indicate that relatives hoped and expected that patients would be cured. Between May 1834 and June 12, 1838, a total of 658 patients received care. Of these, 292 were discharged, 248 died, and 118 remained as of the latter date. Its name changed to Eastern State Hospital, the institution continues to care for the mentally ill today.

John Hunt remained a steadfast supporter of Transylvania University. In 1812, on behalf of the board of trustees, he wrote Henry Clay asking Clay to engage the architect Benjamin Latrobe to draw up plans for a new building. From 1819 to 1835 Hunt served on the board of trustees. During the first eight of these years, the university experienced the enlightened administration of President Horace Holley, a well-known Unitarian minister from Boston. Early in 1818 liberals had overthrown the conservative Presbyterians in control of the institution. Holley and the liberals attempted to develop a great state university, conducted on liberal principles and open to all religious denominations. In the sixteen years before Holley came, 22 students had been graduated. During Holley's nine years (1818–1827), there were 666 graduates, and Transylvania was recognized nationally for outstanding instruction, especially in law and medicine. Hunt and President Holley and their families were close friends. In 1822 Holley wrote John:

"With your friendship for me I am entirely satisfied, and place unreserved confidence in the sincerity and simplicity of your declarations of respect and good will."

In 1827 religious conservatives regained control of Transylvania and Horace Holley left Lexington. Hunt continued as a trustee as did Henry Clay (intermittently), John Bradford, and other prominent Lexingtonians. For six months—between November 20, 1828, and May 23, 1829—Hunt was chairman of the board. He was very active in serving on committees and was particularly valuable in advising on financial and building matters. After fire destroyed the principal building of the university in 1829 he was chairman of the building committee responsible for replacing it. James Morrison, a businessman and former chairman of the board, had left the university a legacy of $70,000 and the new building was to be named for him. The trustees authorized Hunt to commission as its architect Gideon Shryock, a pioneer in bringing Greek revival architecture across the Alleghenies. Construction of the building, hindered by the cholera epidemic of 1833, was completed by November 14, 1833, and the building stands today as a beautiful example of Greek revival architecture.

Hunt continued a leader in the Episcopal church in Lexington. He was vestryman for six years and warden for seven years during the period between 1813 and 1833. Shortly after his death, a former church member wrote to the pastor: "I regret very much to have heard of the death of two of the main pillars in your congregation. It would scarcely seem like old Lexington to me, and especially would it be hard for me to convince myself that I was in the Episcopal Church there, without seeing those two old gentlemen, John Brand [who died shortly before Hunt] and John W. Hunt, in their places before me."

It does not seem that Hunt was ever directly involved in politics. His friend, Henry Clay, sometimes requested business advice, and they had business dealings together. It seems reasonable to suppose that Hunt would have supported Clay and the Whig party. However, in the Hunt papers, only one reference to political activity on the part of Hunt was discovered. In 1840, at a time when he was visiting in Louisville, his name was used as "manager" of a ball given in Lexington for Whig presidential candidate William Henry Harrison.

It is doubtful that Hunt ever felt guilty about the fortune which he had acquired. The climate of opinion of the time approved everything he had done and people had great respect for him. He gave back to society by serving the asylum, Transylvania, and the church. Apparently his largest contribution to charity was the $5,000 which he bequeathed to the Lexington orphans' home.

The years passed and the children left Hopemont. The young ladies attracted prominent young businessmen and lawyers from distant areas. Hunt's eldest daughter, Mary, married John H. Hanna, a lawyer, banker, manufacturer, and for many years clerk for the United States District Court in Frankfort. Theodosia chose Colonel George F. Strother, a lawyer and politician in Saint Louis. Eleanor became the wife of Richard A. Curd, a Lexington attorney. Anne accepted the hand of William B. Reynolds, a Louisville businessman, and lovely Henrietta married Colonel Calvin C. Morgan, a businessman from Huntsville, Alabama.

Two of the boys became lawyers, two merchants and manufacturers, and two physicians. The eldest son, Charlton, was an eloquent and impassioned speaker who developed into one of Kentucky's most prominent lawyers. In 1832 he became the first mayor of the newly incorporated city of Lexington, and he was re-elected in 1833 and 1834. As mayor, he is given credit for founding the city's first public school system. On December 27, 1836, at the age of thirty-five, he died of scarlet fever. After his death, the western part of what was then Water

Street was named "Hunt's Row" in his honor. Francis Key Hunt maintained a law office on Short Street in Lexington, followed in his father's footsteps as chairman of the board of managers of the insane asylum, and was on the law faculty at Transylvania University.

Abraham was graduated from Transylvania and had entered general merchandising in Florence, Alabama, by 1831. In 1836 he took up the wholesale grocery business in New Orleans. The panic of 1837 caused his company to lose money, and by 1840 he had returned to Lexington and was manufacturing hemp products. Later he became a successful banker in Louisville. Thomas H. Hunt was a partner with his father in retail and wholesale merchandising in Lexington between 1834 and 1836. Two years later, Thomas had begun manufacturing bagging and bale rope. After medical school, Robert served as a physician in Lexington.

By 1830 John and Catherine were in their fifties and there were grandchildren to love. When Catherine was in Saint Louis she reported: "Sally is seated by my side and says I must tell Grandpa to send Aunt Anne [for a visit] and Hunt desires his love to Grandfather. The Children are very sweet." Theodosia thanked her mother for the gift of the books Theodosia and her brothers and sisters had enjoyed as children. "We received your . . . letter to-gether with the Books, which have delighted the children so much. They have scarcely been out of their hands since they reached here. And not only were the children pleased the mother too, had a flood of feeling and recollection, started at the sight of books that she had seen in the hands of all, nearly all, her brothers and sisters. They were truly memorials of 'home sweet home.' "

On October 17, 1835, at the age of fifty-seven, Catherine Hunt died at Hopemont. John, now sixty-two, drew closer to the children, especially his daughters. He became extremely generous toward them. Theodosia, a widow in Saint Louis, asked for $300 in 1840 and promptly received $500. When he died large sums had been advanced to the sons and daughters. In 1840 Theodosia wrote: "You my dear father have been the prop and counsellor of a large family and years seem only to add to the sphere of your comprehensive benevolent and most affectionate duties. Few have known so well how to act and still fewer have been so liberal and uniformly kind and affectionate."

They enjoyed joking with him. During a trip to New Orleans Mary stated: "I must tell you on Anne. Every morning I knock at her door at a pretty late hour, to know if she is ready for breakfast. She makes Sarah delay opening the door until she jumps out of bed & the reply is 'not quite.' " From New Orleans Anne sent curtains, tablecloths, and Madras handkerchiefs. "I can see Charles [probably a house servant] puffing over the box. You standing by giving directions, then picking up the different packages & looking at the names."

Tempting him with promises of good food, the sons and daughters begged for a visit. Son-in-law John Hanna in Frankfort promised: "The Strawberries are now in perfection. Will you not make us a visit. . . . Do break off from the ties of home and tarry with us a few days. We will promise at least a hearty welcome, and as for eating the best we can give." Theodosia told him: "Rose [a servant] has cleaned your room and laid up some dried beef and tongue! and hope that some very good coffee I have will hold out till the happy arrival."

And John's grandchildren were devoted to him. Once Sally, Theodosia's daughter in Saint Louis, wrote him a thank-you letter: "The silk dress you gave me has just come from the Dress-maker's. It is most beautiful. I am very much afraid to wear it, for fear of making people sin. I dislike to see any one covetous." She closed with: "I remain, my dear good, sweet, darling, elegant, loving grandpa, your affectionate grand Child."

In his sixties and seventies, during seasonable weather, John rode daily to the farm in Fayette County.

He was sixty-eight in 1841 when daughter Mary reflected: "I suppose before this reaches you, you will have enjoyed a ride over your farm and in addition to the pleasure of seeing your calves & pigs, you have had a sight of rich clover fields. Aye and at last such is the most rational & satisfactory mode of enjoyment." He produced hemp, corn, wheat, and hay, and raised hogs, cattle, and horses. Interested in scientific advances in agriculture, in 1838 he began using a horse-drawn wheat-threshing machine and in 1843 he purchased a steam sawmill. But he was not always successful in his attempts to make improvements. Once his son smiled: "The *orchard grass* in the old cherry orchard has turned out to be a very fine crop of *Fox tail.*"

At sixty-eight John continued to rise early and keep his appointments. William A. Leavy gave an example:

He [Hunt] made an appointment with me to call on me at my farm near Lexn. at an early hour after breakfast in the year 1841 to see my cattle I think *at seven o'clock* as I knew his punctuality, and tried to be ready, but had not finished my breakfast and was not yet expecting him, when he came *a little before the time appointed.* His overseer, Mr. Marrs, told me that he frequently came to his farm and surprised him by his visit *4 miles from town by sunrise;* Patrick Dolan who was very often engaged by him for the purchase of Stock bears the same testimony to his early hours and more than punctuality to his appointment.

John was seventy-six when the cholera epidemic of 1849 swept into Kentucky from New Orleans. In May it broke out in the Lunatic Asylum and in June it spread to the town. Lucretia and Henry Clay were stricken but recovered. By August 18 the pestilence had claimed 342 lives in Lexington. On August 21 John died at Hopemont. The newspaper did not report cholera as the cause of death, but the symptoms ("chronic diarrhoea terminating in flux") indicate that it was.

The Lexington *Observer and Reporter* paid tribute to John:

The deceased was one of our eldest, most estimable citizens, and enjoyed to an unlimited extent the respect and confidence of all who knew him.—He was remarkable for his business qualifications, for great energy of character, for uprightness and integrity in all his transactions, and his loss will be severely felt in our city, in which for half a century he has occupied a most prominent position.

Hunt learned the merchandising trade as a boy from his father, Trenton's most prominent merchant. Abraham was a good teacher. John's older brothers were successful businessmen in Philadelphia and Trenton for years. John's cousin, Wilson P. Hunt, was apprenticed to Abraham and went on to become the chief agent of John Jacob Astor. Unquestionably, Abraham was one of the most influential persons in John's early life.

John was fortunate to be in the right place at the right time. His brothers, Pearson and Wilson, appear to have been fairly competent businessmen but neither achieved John's level of success. Pearson's Philadelphia wholesale business failed in 1804, and he became a bank clerk. Wilson's wholesale and shipping firm in the same city went bankrupt in 1826. John's son Abraham proved to be a proficient businessman later, but the panic of 1837 wiped out his mercantile company in New Orleans. John came to Lexington in 1795, an ideal time and place to launch a career on the urban frontier. Yet other men in the same time and place failed to reach Hunt's level of accomplishment.

Hunt possessed the ability, characteristic of many entrepreneurs, to visualize profit possibilities in new methods, new commodities, and new markets. Delighting in ventures, Hunt had a sense of when to redirect his investments. For example, he was a pioneer in the profitable business of manufacturing cotton bagging in Kentucky, but several years later, in 1814, sold his factory shortly before the industry entered a period of great decline. In 1838 Hunt's stockbroker stated: "You will find by this time that if you did not go into the Stock

Market exactly at the right time, that you were not far wrong, for stocks have been improving every since."

Along with a remarkable sense of when to get into and out of ventures, Hunt possessed the ability to overcome the obstacles standing in the way of accomplishing something new. He appreciated the value of good contacts and connections. Abijah was located in Cincinnati, then in Natchez. John's brothers and father kept him apprised of market conditions and prices and aided him in making credit arrangements in the Northeast. Through the merchant and manufacturing days and on into the time of Hunt's entry into the stock market, their advice and aid were factors in his success. Neighboring businessmen respected his judgment in the choice of agents in distant markets.

John showed exemplary attention to detail and kept nearly all of the operations with which he was concerned under his strict personal control. William Anderson, Andrew Jackson's associate, told him: "You are not only an attentive; but a particular man in the execution of business." He also made a point of giving detailed and clear instructions to his agents and brokers in the South and East. They were never to buy or sell outside the limits which he set. In 1813 he stopped dealing with Hollins & Brown of Baltimore when the commission firm disobeyed his instructions and sold a shipment of yarns at seven months credit instead of four months or less. Not all merchant-manufacturers were as stringent. In 1805 James Weir gave his agent in Natchez authority to sell hemp products below Weir's minimum price. "I think it would be presumption in me," wrote Weir, "to direct or dictate to you in this case, who being on the spot must possess the best information on the subject, and having the highest confidence in your better judgment submit the thing to yourself." In 1808 Weir told his agent in New Orleans: "Make sale to the best advantage for my account." Hunt seldom, if ever, gave as much leeway.

Joseph A. Schumpeter, a Viennese economist, has set forth the theory that innovation is the root cause of economic development. Schumpeter maintained that when entrepeneurs introduce new methods or start new kinds of business ventures, a static economic world becomes dynamic and improvement or progress results. John W. Hunt was an entrepreneur in the Schumpeterian sense; he was an innovator in frontier merchandising, manufacturing, wholesale trading, horse breeding, banking, and insurance. Hunt's career stimulated the spread of population westward, which opened vast areas of fertile land to commercial agriculture. He contributed to the expansion of production and to the over-all growth of the American economy in the antebellum period.

When John Wesley Hunt died, his family's fortune and social position were well established. The position of leadership of the family and prominence in the community occupied by Hunt passed to his grandson, John Hunt Morgan, the Confederate general. Hunt's great grandson, Thomas Hunt Morgan, born at Hopemont, won the Nobel Prize in Physiology and Medicine in 1933 for research in genetics. The Hunts and Morgans would long continue as leaders in the life of Kentucky and the nation.

Bibliographical Essay

B Y FAR THE most valuable source on John Wesley Hunt's life is the large collection of Hunt-Morgan Papers at the Margaret I. King Library, University of Kentucky. The collection contains accounts, invoices, receipts, bills of exchange, bills of lading, memorandums, and correspondence on nearly every aspect of Hunt's life. Among the many detailed accounts are those for the Lexington-Cincinnati trade of the 1790s. There are many family letters, including several written by Catherine Hunt to John. Letters from John's family in Trenton reveal a great deal about life in that city in the 1790s and early 1800s.

The John W. Hunt Papers at the Filson Club in Louisville contain documents on Hunt's mercantile, horse breeding, manufacturing, trading and financial activities, as well as many family letters. The collection includes several bills of sale for slaves and contains valuable information on Hunt's children. The John W. Hunt Papers at the Transylvania University library are a particularly valuable source on Hunt as a financier. There are many letters relating to his stock investments and family matters. For detailed references to these collections and other sources see James A. Ramage, "The Hunts and Morgans: A Study of a Prominent Kentucky Family," Ph.D. dissertation, University of Kentucky, 1972.

The Dandridge Papers in the Cincinnati Historical Society Library shed light on the Cincinnati-Lexington trade and make clear that Abijah Hunt was a principal army supplier. The Hunt Papers at the Missouri Historical Society Library and the Abijah and David Hunt Papers at the Mississippi Department of Archives and History contain information on Hunt. Material on Abraham Hunt was obtained at the Free Public Library in Trenton, New Jersey. The nature of Abraham's business is revealed in correspondence in the William Tilghman Papers, The Historical Society of Pennsylvania and the Stephen Girard Papers, The American Philosophical Society Library.

Newspapers were an important source. Advertisements and articles in the *Kentucky Gazette* of Lexington were of great value. Other Lexington newspapers were the *Kentucky Reporter, Reporter, Observer and Reporter,* and the *American Statesman.* Knowledge of the Hunt prominence in early Cincinnati was obtained from *The Centinel of the North-Western Territory, Freeman's Journal,* and *The Western Spy and Hamilton Gazette,* all published in Cincinnati. These papers show Cincinnati trade with northern Kentucky, but not with Lexington. *The Spirit of the Times* reported Hunt's interest in the trotter horse.

Among the sources studied to evaluate Hunt's role in relation to other area merchants and manufacturers, the following were valuable: James Wier [sic] Letterbooks, Draper Manuscripts, Kentucky, Vol. 20, microfilm at King Library, University of Kentucky, original at State Historical Society of Wisconsin; John Brand Letterbook, microfilm at the University of Kentucky, original the property of Henry Duncan of Lexington; Thomas Dye Owings Papers at the University of Kentucky; Dwight L. Smith, ed., *The Western Journals of John May: Ohio Company Agent and Business Adventurer* (Cincinnati, 1961); Lexington Tax Assessment Book, 1796–1806, Draper Manuscripts, Kentucky, Vol. 20; Lexington Tax Assessment Books, City Hall, Lexington; Lexington Trustees Book, 1781–1811, photocopy in King Library, University of Kentucky, original in Lexington City Hall; and Kentucky, State Tax Records, microfilm at Kentucky

Historical Society Library, Frankfort, Kentucky. The letterbooks of James Weir are a valuable source, but they give an incomplete picture of Weir's business. For example, there are no extant entries for the period between July 1806 and April 1808. The correspondence of John Brand is useful but does not cover the period before 1811. One of the values of the Hunt papers is that they document Hunt's early entry into the manufacture of cotton bagging.

Contributory to an understanding of the role of pioneer merchants were: Lewis E. Atherton, *The Frontier Merchant in Mid-America* (Columbia, Missouri, 1971); Atherton, *The Southern Country Store, 1800–1860* (Baton Rouge, 1949); Margaret E. Martin, *Merchants and Trade of the Connecticut River Valley, 1750–1820* (Northampton, Massachusetts, 1939); and Marietta Jennings, *A Pioneer Merchant of St. Louis, 1810–1820* (New York, 1939).

Particularly useful secondary sources included: James F. Hopkins, *A History of the Hemp Industry in Kentucky* (Lexington, 1951); Robert S. Starobin, *Industrial Slavery in the Old South* (New York, 1970); John Hervey, *The American Trotter* (New York, 1947); John G. Clark, *New Orleans, 1718–1812; An Economic History* (Baton Rouge, 1970); Richard V. Clemence, *The Schumpeterian System* (Cambridge, 1950). An excellent study of Kentucky banking is Dale M. Royalty, "Banking, Politics, and the Commonwealth, Kentucky, 1800–1825," Ph.D. dissertation, University of Kentucky, 1971.

There is no analytical history of Lexington. The following were useful: William H. Perrin, *History of Fayette County, Kentucky* (Chicago, 1882); George W. Ranck, *History of Lexington* (Cincinnati, 1872); and Richard H. Collins, *History of Kentucky . . .* (Kentucky Historical Society edition, 2 vols., Frankfort, 1966). William A. Leavy provides a special contemporary view of Hunt and Lexington in "Memoir of Lexington and Its Vicinity," *The Register of the Kentucky Historical Soci-*

ety 40 (April, July, 1942), 107–131; and 41 (January, 1943), 44–62. *The Papers of Henry Clay* (5 vols. to date, Lexington, 1959–), edited by James F. Hopkins and Mary W. M. Hargreaves, provide valuable primary material and reveal a great deal about prominent individuals in Lexington and Kentucky. Richard C. Wade, *The Urban Frontier: The Rise of Western Cities, 1790–1830* (Cambridge, 1959) shows the relationship of Lexington to other towns on the frontier. Temple Bodley and Samuel M. Wilson, *History of Kentucky* (4 vols., Chicago, 1928) and William E. Connelly and E. Merton Coulter, *History of Kentucky*, Charles Kerr, ed. (5 vols., Chicago, 1922) were also consulted.